THE HOLY SPIRIT

SO...WHAT'S THE BIG DEAL?

by

JERRY COOK

ISBN: 148233061X
ISBN 13: 9781482330618
Library of Congress Control Number: 2013903414
CreateSpace Independent Publishing Platform
North Charleston, SC

Table of Contents

———➤———

Introduction

"So...What's the big deal?"

I was in a conversation with a young pastor who was struggling with the subject of the Holy Spirit and the idea of speaking in tongues in particular. My first reaction (unspoken, thank God) was,

"How dare you! Who do you think you are to question the ministry and expressions of the Holy Spirit? You're a pastor and you want to know what the "big deal" is?"

When I aborted my little inner tirade, I realized this was an important question which deserved a reasonable answer. Really now, what *is* the big deal? When you consider all the foolishness and extremes that have swirled around it, a case can be made for abandoning the subject to neutral generalities. No loving pastor wants to lead his congregation down the path to excess or fanaticism. As a serious Christian I certainly want to receive everything Christ intends, but I sure don't want to be strange or goofy.

I have been a pastor for 50 years; half a century. (And I'm so young!) I have seen excesses come and go in every conceivable format. I must admit, however, at times even I am shocked by some new twist on an old theme. My position often has simply been, "This too shall pass." But, my young friend doesn't have the benefit of the longer view. Perhaps he has seen out of control behavior and odd "manifestations," attributed to the Holy Spirit, which were shocking and distasteful to him. The good, the bad and the ugly were all jumbled up together and spit out in the name of the Holy Spirit.

Yes! Absolutely! He must be given a clear sensible and Biblical answer. That answer is the intention of this book.

Here is a short list of what not to expect:

1. This is not an exhaustive treatise on the Holy Spirit.

2. This is not a research paper complete with footnotes and mountains of references.

3. This is not a formal theology book. It will deal with subjects of theological importance but not the minute details of theology.

4. This is not an academic, theoretical work. It is academically valid and correct. However, I am not in the least interested in the theoretical

Ok. Now what *can* you expect?

1. **Honesty**: I will share a bit of my own struggles, doubts and questions as I have lived with this "big deal."

2. **Practicality**: Can serious Christians experience the fullness of the Holy Spirit including speaking in tongues without becoming a religious nut? Why would they want to? If so, how?

3. **Viewpoint**: What does my belief about God (my theology) look like when viewed from the Day of Pentecost as its center-point?

4. **Hope**: It is possible to be a sane, intellectually honest, Biblical and dynamic Christian who is filled with the Holy Spirit, speaks in tongues and effectually ministers the full life of Christ.

You bet it is "a big deal" and here's why:

PART ONE
Six Events That Changed the World

The In-breaking of God

———◆———

Where is your God? Where do you send your prayers? When you ask Him to come, where does He come from?

I am sometimes invited to bring the prayer at the opening of our State Legislative session. "Dr. Cook will now bring the Invocation," it is announced. That means, I am supposed to invite God to join in the meeting of our state law-makers. Now, if He should decide to come, where does He come from? What if He doesn't want to come? Or, perhaps more poignant, what if He actually shows up?

For many, God is just generally on duty out there someplace. He is close enough to be comforting but far enough to not be disturbing. Even some of our songs plead with the God out there to come over here, get me over there or at least designate a place to meet half way.

It did not start this way. In the story of our beginnings, the book of Genesis, we see a God who is very much *with* us. He, in fact, created us and breathed life into our clay nostrils. We strolled through the garden with Him at the close of every day. It is a grand picture of a God enjoying His creation and His creation enjoying their Creator. Only in our wildest imagination can we construct what it would be like to be in touch every evening with our Creator. As much as we anticipate the return of our lover, or a son from a long absence, or a parent's welcome home -- all of that pales in comparison to the glorious moment for Adam and Eve when He came in the cool evening time. Their longing for Him was so intense that it still aches deep inside us.

In those evening walks, our first parents learned who they were and why they had been created. From their Maker they learned their destiny and what the future in partnership with Him would be like. All of this and much more was expanded and unveiled for them in Divine disclosure every evening. Its glory was stamped deeply in all succeeding generations.

But something cosmically catastrophic happened. He stopped coming and the way to Him was sealed up and guarded by angels with flaming swords. However, the longing -- the ache inside for Him to come not only remained, it became unbearable. Without our evening fellowship with Him, our confident sense of identity dissipated like a morning mist. Our purpose was lost. Our future became unsafe and foreboding like a venture in a strange forest at night with the moon hidden and only the fearful night sounds as company. No Godly presence. The knowledge that we were loved or even lovable slipped away. We then began to corrupt all our efforts to love.

The Garden was gone and our world became an enemy. It resisted our every effort. The animals we had named and trusted became our stalkers. The ground mocked us with thorns. Our children became rebellious, even murderous.

If only He would come again this evening ... but evening after evening, year after century -- He never came. Memories of our Garden slipped farther away with every generation, like a ship we hoped would rescue us melting away in the horizon leaving only a blot on our memory. Finally, even the blot was gone and we doubted there had ever been a ship -- a Garden -- a God who walked with us.

But why did He suddenly abandon us?

That question is not answerable. It is framed wrong. Have you noticed that is the way with questions? If they are not posed just right they cannot be answered. When we seek to find out why He abandoned us we float aimlessly in one of two directions. We did something to drive Him away and we therefore must find some way to change His mind. Or, He was never really there in the first place, so suck it up and do the best you can with the mess life has become.

However, if we tweak the question just a little bit, answers become possible. Isn't it amazing how we can struggle for an answer so hard and never examine the actual question? Always question the question when you are struggling for an answer. For example, something as simple as changing, "What's wrong with her?" to, "What's wrong with me?" can bring up whole new avenues to pursue.

By changing the question, "Why has God abandoned me?" to "Why have I abandoned Him?" gives us the possibility of answers. We are now dealing with our own action, which we can change, rather than His action, which we cannot. You see, if He has rejected us, we have no hope. It is His move and we can't manipulate or beg Him into making it. He is God, after all. But if *we* have rejected *Him* and if He is welcoming to us, there is hope.

Let's go back to the Garden for a minute. There is a conversation that we need to listen to carefully.

One day, before their evening walk with God, our first parents had a conversation with a beautiful serpent. Basically, without going into the whole exchange, he lied to them. He convinced them that their evening companion was not the friend he appeared to be. He was represented as only toying with them, cheating them out of knowing what was really going on. The serpent persuaded them that he was really their friend and the God they had been spending their evenings with was their enemy.

That afternoon they abandoned their walk and hid from their companion.

With that disastrous choice our parents abandoned God and chose to believe and worship the beautiful creature. Only too late did they discover the serpent was in fact, Satan in disguise. They had been kidnapped and sold into the slavery of rebellion. A rebellion that this very Satan had begun in heaven, for which he was driven out and barred from entrance. Now, he had deceived the objects of God's greatest love and they joined the excommunicated ranks of Satan himself.

That fatal choice injected the venom of rebellion into the very DNA of Adam, his wife Eve, and all future generations. Its infection passed through their descendants and became known as "the sinful nature." In Romans 5, the Apostle Paul writes about it when he says, "In Adam all sinned."

Now, let's come back to our question of the location of God. Remember, He started *with* us. He was our creator and evening companion. We have now joined the rebellion and have relegated Him to "out there." He is not "out there" in terms of His cosmic location, but in terms of our relationship with Him. It is this breach of relationship that the Bible deals with. It describes the process whereby He re-enters our reality. It traces the plan He masterfully constructs; the pathway into our rebellious hearts, and offers us the possibility of escape from Satan's slavery.

Life with Satan was horrific. Nothing was like he led us to believe. Everything God cultivated in us during our times together was perverted or destroyed. We lost any sense of who we were, why we were, or where we were. We were trapped in a vicious cycle just trying to survive. And, there was this incredible pain and longing inside: The vague sense that it had not always been this way. We tried to silence the inner turmoil with every conceivable (and some inconceivable) thing. When the need to worship became unbearable, we tried to create our own gods just to get something bigger, something out there to help. We begged our gods to help us, we even sacrificed our children to them, but they mocked us in mute ineptness. Even our need for love betrayed us and turned instead to an insatiable, appetite driven sexuality that debased us and made us hate ourselves and everyone else.

The Old Testament describes how God began to break into this cosmic disaster. He came to our slavery and His coming was not in the least abstract. It was concrete. He created again, only this time not just a man and woman but an entire nation. Israel. His chosen people.

This tiny nation became the sound stage for the incredible presentation redemption. Just like us, God created her for Himself. Through rebellion she was captured and enslaved. But her story does not end there as ours did. She was delivered from slavery and led to the Promised Land. On this stage we see the story of every nation -- of every man -- of humankind.

The "God out there" roars into action.

"Set my people free!" He demands of Pharaoh, and the story of a pursuing God, a reluctant man, and a stubborn devil begins. But it is more. It is the story of redemption, freedom and hope. And what a story it is! It is the voice of this almighty God blazing into human history in fire and power and wonders never before seen. He crushes the non-gods of our own making. He destroys the myths that tell us there are many gods, angry gods, promiscuous gods enshrined in our fallen appetites; voracious gods demanding even our infants as a sacrifice to be consumed in their flaming bellies. We endured all this pain as we begged for good crops, crops which seldom came. Good years were always put off until the next tragic sacrifice.

Our impotent gods collapsed at the voice of this God and the anthem of His people became, "OUR GOD IS ONE GOD... ABOVE HIM THERE IS NO OTHER.

He was still out there, but we knew without doubt that He was indeed "There!" And, even more exciting, He wanted us to rejoin Him, to resume fellowship again. He was inviting us to come out of hiding and walk with Him. But, there was the horrible canyon of our rebellion. All our attempts to build a bridge to Him collapsed into a chasm of helpless despair. That is the dilemma in the Old Testament but the dilemma is mollified by a subtle theme -- a promise keeps whispering. A Messiah: A Redeemer who would deliver His people from their sin and bring us again to our Father.

However, so much more had to be known before He could come. We had to learn something of God's ways. What were His thoughts about us? What did He see when He looked at us? We couldn't just kiss and make up. That's fairytale stuff and this is certainly no fairytale. And, the rebellion--something had to be done about the rebellion.

In preparation for this Deliverer of Israel, and through her all mankind, God gave an elaborate system of laws, feasts and celebrations and of sacrifices and rituals. Through these we began to understand; "His thoughts are not our thoughts. His ways are not our ways." Through them we learn of His glory and power. We learn the incredible depth of our sin and the gigantic cost of our redemption. We learn that changed behavior does not change our heart and the blood of lambs could not cleanse our soul. He revealed Himself to this little nation and *all* the nations watched in awe.

Israel learned to love the laws and ways of this One God. She learned to worship Him and nothing, or no one, else. She came to Him for forgiveness and saw the extreme cost of reconciliation. Sacrifice was needed to wrench the captives from their vicious slave master. The wages of sin is indeed death, and someone had to die. But it couldn't be one of us. Not even a good and big one of us. Rebellion was in our DNA and it had hopelessly carved its demented ways into our very soul.

We all cry as Israel cries, "Create in me a clean heart, Oh God, and renew a right spirit within me."[1]

---

1   Psalm 51

The Incarnation

———————

In the last chapter we realized that if we are ever to have a renewed relationship with God, He must initiate it. He began by breaking into our reality and showing His great longing to be with us. He also explained the catastrophic distance our rebellion caused. We have no way to get to Him, so if we are ever to do more than just know *about* Him, if we are ever to *know* Him, He must come to us. But, how is this all-powerful God going to come to us? Our Jewish ancestors were so terrified of Him they would not even pronounce His name and believed that if they were ever to see Him face-to-face they would die.

There is a remarkable event that illustrates this. It is when Moses had gone up to the mountain to receive the Ten Commandments.

And the Lord said, "I will cause all my goodness to pass in front of you, and I will proclaim my name, the Lord, in your presence. I will have mercy on whom I will have mercy, and I will have compassion on whom I will have compassion. But," he said, "You cannot see my face, for no one may see me and live." Then the Lord said, "There is a place near me where you may stand on a rock. When my glory passes by, I will put you in a cleft in the rock and cover you with my hand until I have passed by. Then I will remove my hand and you will see my back; but my face must not be seen." [2]

Not only is this God terrifying and unapproachable, He is not human! He is not merely a big one of us. He can't just arrive on the scene and introduce himself. Or...can He? What if He did?

Well, He can and He did.

Can you imagine a less intimidating entrance than to be born as a baby? Though angels and special stars and heavenly choirs accompanied His birth, the baby was not found in a palace or a shrine erected especially for the event. He was in a sheep shed, wrapped in common cloths with a teenage mother holding Him. His much older stepfather (God was His father), Joseph, watched in astonishment as the marvel unfolded.

God entered our world exactly the same way we do ... as a baby. We held Him. We pinched His cheeks to make Him laugh. We had no idea we were holding God! Only Mary, His mother, knew and she kept it all in her young heart.

There was nothing remarkable about his first twelve years. He grew like all other children. He played and laughed and probably had to learn a few parental lessons along the way. His early years were so normal they are not even mentioned in his biographies. It wasn't until he was twelve years old that His life began to veer away from the path of other children.

He had gone with his parents to Jerusalem for a great celebration. When it was over and everyone left for home, He stayed behind to converse with the teachers in the Temple. He astounded these learned experts with his questions and some of his ideas. When Mary asked why He had not come with them when everyone left for home, He gave the first hint of his true mission. Until that time He had been about his stepfather's carpentry business. He now announced, "I must be about *my* "father's business."

2 Exodus 34:19-23

Interestingly, the next eighteen years were spent working with Joseph in the carpenter's shop, where He learned the very human lesson of becoming a man.

In his thirtieth year, everything changed. He was now considered an adult by his culture -- a true man. Now He began to reveal that He was not just fully a man but fully God. He was acting not only as a man, He was acting as and for *Mankind*! He was man as God intended. But He was also God. Through him we were not only to see the real man, but we would see the real God! Matthew, Mark, Luke and John are eyewitnesses who actually lived the events and recorded them for us all.

He said he had come to "Show us the Father." That's the exclusive way He referred to God: "The Father," "Our Father," "My Father." Whenever Jesus talks about God it is always, "Father." That is the first thing He wants us to know: God is *fatherly*. He is everything a perfect father could be, and more.

We have never seen a perfect father. All our fathers, no matter how loving, are flawed, some more than others. All our families are dysfunctional. He began to show us what our perfect Father God is like and it is astounding. This God is not anything like the pagan gods they made and worshipped fearfully in their shrines and temples.

Man's idea of God, whatever form it took, was that He was full of anger. He didn't like us and was just looking for any chance to cause us problems and punish us. Gods were angry, promiscuous, and violent -- they were just big ones of us. But this Jesus is entirely different.

He is not angry!

How can this be? He sees our hatred and our evil. He sees the planet that we have ravaged. He hears us swearing and witnesses our baseness. If He is God he should really be full of rage! But He isn't. He certainly doesn't ignore our evil. He confronts it wherever it expresses itself, but He never reacts punitively. He is not looking for someone to punish, it seems that He is looking for someone to forgive... someone to heal. He seems to care for us.

Many of the things He does and says are not very god-like He does wonderful miracles but insists on doing them on the wrong day and this invites the rage of the religious leaders. He doesn't speak in riddles or mysteries like the old pagan gods, or even with the vagueness of our own teachers. Everything He says rings true. Even if you don't agree you have to admit, even marvel at His authority. He knows what He is talking about!

We always assumed that God, or the gods, were responsible for both the good and evil in the world. But, this Man only did *good*. He never destroyed anything, never made healthy people sick or brought death to the living. Quite the opposite. His touch healed and His voice calmed the storm. Could God really be like this?

He said, "I have not come to be served..." What an astonishing statement for God to make. Even today we learn from an early age that you serve God and that He rewards those who do and punishes those who don't.

"If you haven't come to be served, then why have you come?"

His answer opens a whole new world to us. "I have not come to be served, but to serve and give my life for you."[3]

He has come to serve me? What can He mean? My mind goes back to the times he asked, "What do you want me to do for you?"

The lepers.

The man at the pool.

I call it the "Jesus question." What can I do for you? Do you see what this does? Suddenly, the power and life of God is made available to us. He steps into our pain, our suffering, our brokenness and asks, "Is there anything I can do for you?"

---

3   Matthew 20:28

On a dusty road with crowds following Him and people trying to silence the obnoxious blind beggar who kept screaming for His attention:

"What do you want me to do for you?" He asks.

Jesus, isn't it obvious? The man is blind! But how many people can you ask to give you new eyes? All of his begging for those many years and there never had been anyone he could ask for the one thing he ached for every minute of every day. But here He was!

"I want to see," he begs.

So Jesus gave him new eyes! His first light revealed the face of Jesus, of God. All the theological explanations of why he was blind crumbled in shattered foolishness. God was here to bring sight to the blind, not to punish the seeing with blindness. He was here to serve us -- to save us, not to demand our servitude.

If Jesus is God, it's too good to be true. But it is true. The shouts of Hosanna echo throughout Jerusalem when He finally comes to the Holy City. He rides on a colt in royal fashion; His pathway paved with palm branches and hundreds singing His praises.

But the City of Peace was not to be the place of His Coronation. It was the place of His cruel, tortuous execution.

EVENT 3

The Death of Jesus

And, we executed Him!

We chose Barabbas, a highwayman who had done no good, over a Savior who had done *only* good.[4] We were blinded by jealousy, hatred and misplaced zeal. Again we chose the snake over the Son.

Why am I using "we" to talk about these things? It happened long ago and far away. I know. I like to think I would have been among the weeping disciples mourning His death. But, when I listen carefully inside, somewhere in that crowd I hear my voice jeering, "Crucify Him." It is my sins that brought Him here. I cannot stand aloof and hide behind a curtain of the ages.

God had indeed broken in. He had lived with us for thirty-three years and again we abandoned Him. To his executioners, good riddance. Death had won. However, there is much more going on here. This is the death of "Humankind." The Apostle Paul says definitively, "I am crucified with Christ," [5] then he builds his theology on the fact that we are all buried with Him in baptism and raised with Him to new life in His resurrection. This

---

4   Acts 10:38 NIV

5   Galatians 2:20

death of Jesus is not just a recorded historical fact it is a universal event! In Christ's death fallen man is paid his wages: Death.

Indeed, "It is finished," as He cried from the cross. He is not referring to the suffering being over and the numbness of death finally coming. He is talking about the snake, about our rebellion, about fallen man's redemption being paid at last and the slaves set free. The seed of the woman has crushed the serpent's head.[6] At this moment, Satan's power of death is broken because in Jesus, mankind has truly died.

But, He did not just die as mankind; He was the Divine Son of God dying. But can Deity die? Here is the wonder of the Incarnation. He was *fully* God and *fully* man. He was fully man when He died; He was fully divine when He died. This divine Son of God is the one John writes about in his Gospel, "In Him was life."[7] That doesn't mean only that He was alive. It means that life resided *in Him.* He is the source of life. Death was the end of Adam's race, but it was the beginning of a whole new race whose near ancestor was Jesus and the Father He revealed. "In Adam all die, in Christ, all are made alive."[8] We are no longer sons of Adam. Jesus was fully human, but not a son of Adam. He was a fully human Son of God. In Him a new race began. A new family of origin becomes possible for us.

What about Satan and his imps? What did the death of Christ signify for them? There is a marvelous poem written in 1774 by the German poet, Goethe. Here is a poignant section of his description of Satan's plight:

> *On high His victor-banner blows;*
> *E'en angels at His fury quake,*
> *When Christ to the dread judgment goes.*
> *Now speaks He, and His voice is thunder,*

---

6   See Genesis 3:14

7   John 1:4

8   1Cor. 15:22

He speaks; the rocks are rent in sunder,
His breath is like devouring flames.
Thus speaks He: "Tremble, ye accurs'd!
He who from Eden hurl'd you erst,
Your kingdom's overthrow proclaims.
Look up! My children once were ye,
Your arms against Me then ye turn'd,
Ye fell, that ye might sinners be,
Ye've now the wages that ye earn'd.
"My greatest foeman from that day,
Ye led my dearest friends astray,--
As ye had fallen, man must fall.
To kill him evermore ye sought,
'They all shall die the death,' ye thought;
But howl! for Me I won them all.
For them alone did I descend,
For them pray'd, suffer'd, perish'd I.
Ye ne'er shall gain your wicked end;
Who trusts in Me shall never die.

(Thoughts on Jesus Christ's Descent into Hell:
A poem by Goethe, 1764)

So much has been written about this incredible event. It has inspired prose, poetry, music, novels, art, as no other event has. But as horrible the suffering or passionate the hatred or wrenching the grief, as much as I weep before the cross, the message is astoundingly clear. A new age has come! A new Divine option is now here. We can be "born again."

EVENT 4

The Resurrection

"Why do you look for the living among the dead?"[9]

That question could write our history. We stood for centuries at the shrines of our dead gods begging them to be alive, to speak, to prophesy, to act....Do something! But they never did. We left their temples filled with our relics but with no sign of life. This is different. Frighteningly so!

"He is not here. He is risen."

Those words had never been spoken before. Never even the hint of a resurrected god. Our pagan gods had no life to start with and we saw the One we thought was God, die.

"He's gone ahead of you into Jerusalem!"

"The women have seen the Lord!"

Peter brushes John aside and bursts into the tomb...empty! Only a cloth that had covered his face and the grave clothes folded on the sepulcher's stone bench.

Mary saw Him at the garden tomb. She thought it was the gardener. He was seen by 500 at one time.

"Were not our hearts burning within us while he talked with us on the road and opened the Scriptures to us?" recalled the disciples after their walk on the Emmaus road.

---

9   For Biblical account see Luke 24

His followers huddled together; afraid the Jewish leaders would find them and kill them as they had Jesus. Though not as notorious, they were easily identified as his disciples. The windows were shut. The door was locked. Suddenly, He was there! Is it really Him or are we seeing a ghost? (Strange how illogical a terrified mind can become.)

"Look at my hands, my head, my side."

"Oh, my Lord and my God!" Thomas exclaims for them all.

"Peter, do you love me?"

"Yes, Lord."

One denial forgiven and forgotten.

"Peter, do you love me?"

"Yes, Lord."

Two denials forgiven and forgotten.

"Peter, do you love me?"

"Lord, you know..."

Three denials forgiven, forgotten, never to characterize that young man's life again.

He Is Risen...

He Is Risen Indeed!

Had it been the resurrection of only one man, it would have been history's most unique hour. But it was much more. Here, is the beginning of an entirely new race. Not the old fallen mankind who had died three days earlier, but one not tainted by Adam's sin or polluted by his corrupted, rebellious DNA. The grand Divine Option is here. We can be "born again!"

"As in Adam all died, so in Christ all are made alive."

Jesus opened the Old Testament Scriptures to them. Wouldn't we love to have been there! He disclosed himself in the writings of Moses and the prophets. What a Bible study that must have been! He showed them how these last chaotic, horrible, wonderful days had been clearly prophesied in their Scriptures. He was the promised Savior of which the Old Testament whispered. From that education, Christian theology took shape and was proclaimed by all those who attended. It was indeed, good news. It was The Gospel.

Peter, James, John and Paul proclaim the reality of a new race, a new kingdom, a new nation. One not corrupted by sin or separated from God. One re-created in Christ and reconciled to God.

But, it is left to Paul to trumpet it through the ages. "He died; we died. He lives; we live." Jesus had indeed risen from the dead.

"If we have been united with Him in a death like His, we will certainly also be united with Him in a resurrection like His."[10]

He is risen indeed!

---

10 Romans 6:5 NIV

The Ascension

———

"They stood gaping into heaven!"

I would think so. Have you ever been in a conversation and had the person you're talking with start lifting up off the planet? Well, the disciples hadn't seen anything like that either.

Then, two angels in white clothes appeared (who evidently see people floating through the air all the time), and asked them;

"Why are you standing here staring (gaping) into heaven? Jesus has been taken from you into heaven..."[11]

That's the whole problem! He's gone!

Their times together since his resurrection had given them very little to work with:

"I am going away."

"Where are you going?"

"You can't come."

"What should we do?"

"Go tell the whole world about me."

"How do we manage that?"

"The Holy Spirit will show you."

"Where do we find Him?"

"Go back to Jerusalem. He'll find you."

———

11 See Acts 1 for the story of the ascension

...And He left!

With a lot more questions than answers, they hurriedly covered the half-mile to Jerusalem and joined the others I suppose they tried to tell them what had happened but how do you do that?

Remember, the followers of Jesus were still afraid that the authorities would come for them next. The same leaders who killed Jesus had bribed the soldiers guarding His tomb. They ordered them to spread the lie that the disciples had stolen his body. These disciples were not about to start, "being His witnesses in Jerusalem."

It is important to note that the resurrection was *powerful*, but it did not *empower* anyone. The followers of Jesus were hiding behind closed doors after, as well as before, the resurrection. Far from empowering them, it further indicted them. They were not just His followers; they were body snatchers as well!

(A little aside)

It is interesting to me that whenever the Church through the centuries went boldly in her own strength and ingenious plans instead of allowing the Holy Spirit to come to her, she either cowed in fear behind the doors of her institutions, or joined the power structures of the fallen world. Without the Holy Spirit she was like a lion with no teeth, growl but no bite. She growls at Charlemagne and succeeds in making herself into a political structure with no redemptive bite. She growls at paganism and is tamed by the pagan rather than discipling the lost. She growls at atheism and is jeered as an uneducated fool. She snarls at modernism and is mocked as unreasonable. She bares her toothless gums at post-modernism and is dismissed out of hand. Currently, even Christians tend to go running after the latest events or meetings where the Holy Spirit is doing a "new thing." They, too, become a toothless growl and their promise melts away.

But, if you listen carefully you will hear another sound, like the brush of wings just out of sight. Not a lion, not a warrior, not a powerful figure, not a growl, not a snarl, but ...a Dove. Wherever He lights, life happens, hope springs, eyes see and ears hear. He doesn't bare toothless gums and rage. The Dove gently persuades. He transforms those who see and welcome Him and they begin to talk and act and love like Jesus.

But first, before we go further down this road, let's go back to the days between the Ascension and the Holy Spirit's coming. Why did Jesus have to leave in the first place? Why not stay and direct this worldwide mission himself? Well, it is important that we understand a little more about his mission. His plan was not only to multiply his followers, but to *multiply Himself through his followers*. Remember, God's intention in this redemptive journey is to have a new creation in whom He would dwell -- not just *with*, but *in*. So, there is one more step necessary in this incredible adventure from Paradise to Fellowship.

It is detailed in the book of Hebrews. This letter is written to Jewish believers to help them understand that Jesus was their promised Messiah. He was the one whispering throughout their history. The writer draws on their holy symbols that were made concrete in Jesus. The tabernacle, the sacrifices, the shed blood, the feasts, the celebrations, the priesthood, the High priest -- it was all about Jesus. The Book of Hebrews puts it together.

I want to focus on one of these liturgical events. It is the entrance of the High Priest into the very presence of God, the Holy of Holies. There he sprinkles the sacrificial blood on the top of the Ark of the Covenant called the mercy seat. The broken tablets of the law lay beneath; the eyes of God pierced it from above and revealed our sin. But, the blood covered the mercy seat; God no longer saw the broken law of our rebellion. The blood of the sacrifice covered it.

That was the *old*. Hebrews describes, with dramatic artistry, the *new*. Jesus, as our High Priest, ascends into the actual presence of God and presents His own blood at the throne, the place of executive decision for all universes: Not the blood of a goat or lamb or bird -- *His own blood.*

In the ninth chapter of this amazing book, (you must read it for yourself!), the writer talks about a last will and testament, also called a covenant. The one making the will covenants with his descendants that the inheritance will be administered according to his wishes, after his death is certified.

The way we certify a death today is by a death certificate signed by the proper authority. The will can then be opened and the inheritance distributed to the heirs. In the days of the Bible, bringing a sample of the dead person's blood to a court of law certified death. Then the last will and testament, the terms of the covenant, would be carried out by the mediator to the heirs.

The rebellious race of Adam was under a death sentence. That was Satan's wonderful inheritance for them. The blood of animals could not certify their death -- only the blood of mankind. And, the death of Jesus was the death of mankind. The human blood was brought to the court of the universe. The death was certified. Satan's hold was broken! The New Covenant instigated at the last supper is fulfilled:

In the same way, after the supper he took the cup, saying, "This cup is the new covenant in my blood, which is poured out for you."[12]

Here is the wonder! Not only has there been the death of an old race, Adam's, there has been the creation of a new race: The "Sons of God," created "In Christ." The Ascension is indeed an event that changed the world.

The Divine Option. The Grand Choice. Of course Adam's race still inhabits the earth -- but it is a dead race. All of its greatest efforts are doomed because Jesus died. He presented the blood. Their future is set -- death!

12 Luke 29:20 NLT

But now there is a new option. Jesus not only died, but He ascended to the universal court of God, proved the death of Adam's race and opened the way for a new covenant to all who would decide to change families. We now have the choice to leave a race that is dying and be, if you will, "born again."

"Now we are the Sons of God!" Paul proclaims the radical good news. There is HOPE!

Do you see the steps of this journey from rebellion to relationship, from abandonment to fellowship? Transformed from a wicked, tortured, enslaved, twisted creature, hardly recognizable as God's creation to this remarkable new man, with a new heart, a new spirit, a new life -- a New Race.

Do you see it? It's called the Gospel! The Good News! We can be redeemed. We can be reconciled. We can be forgiven and cleansed. It is the message for which the world has pled since the snake first hissed from the tree. None of our gods could answer our plea. But God, Our Savior, Our Christ -- He has accomplished it. He has declared it.

But the only people who know it
are huddled behind closed doors
in Jerusalem
afraid for their lives!

The Day of pentecost

On the day of Pentecost all the believers were meeting together in one place. Suddenly, there was a sound from heaven like the roaring of a mighty windstorm, and it filled the house where they were sitting. Then, what looked like flames or tongues of fire appeared and settled on each of them. And everyone present was filled with the Holy Spirit and began speaking in other languages, as the Holy Spirit gave them this ability.

At that time there were devout Jews from every nation living in Jerusalem. When they heard the loud noise, everyone came running, and they were bewildered to hear their own languages being spoken by the believers.

They were completely amazed. "How can this be?" they exclaimed. "These people are all from Galilee, and yet we hear them speaking in our own native languages! ...They stood there amazed and perplexed. "What can this mean?" they asked each other.

But others in the crowd ridiculed them, saying, "They're just drunk, that's all!" 13

---

13 See Acts 2:1-13 (NLT)

The fear is gone!

No more hushed conversations

No more cowering behind closed doors.

These believers not only went public, they went public with the volume on max. Nearly everyone in Jerusalem heard the commotion and ran to the sound.

What is going on?

They are talking in our native dialects!

They are praising their God!

They are drunk! (As if drunken people usually praised God in languages they had never learned.)

This sudden event is the sixth event that forever changed the world. It is the point to which all the others lead. Death is buried, forgiveness has been granted. We can be redeemed. We can be transformed and made clean. At last we can receive again the holy presence of our God; our Creator. The flaming swords guarding us from Him have become an inner fire which proclaims that the entrance of the Garden is open again. All who will can come in.

What an incredible day! The ages have groaned for it. The prophets predicted it without understanding what they were predicting.

But wait just a minute.

Slow down!

Weren't these disciples present when Jesus came to the locked room and identified himself after the Resurrection?

Yes they were.

And didn't they receive the Holy Spirit then?

You are right. Let's look at it.

*That Sunday evening the disciples were
meeting behind locked doors because they
were afraid of the Jewish leaders. Suddenly,
Jesus was standing there among them!
"Peace be with you," he said. As he spoke,*

he showed them the wounds in his hands
and his side. They were filled with joy when
they saw the Lord! Again he said, "Peace be
with you. As the Father has sent me, so I am
sending you." Then he breathed on them and
said, "Receive the Holy Spirit. If you forgive
anyone's sins, they are forgiven. If you do not
forgive them, they are not forgiven." [14]

There are two key words here; "breathed" and "forgiven."

"He breathed on them..." Do you remember far back in the garden of our first creation? He formed, literally sculpted, man out of the dirt. And do you remember He *"breathed into man the breath of life"*?[15] But that life had been kidnapped and squandered, running with the snake. It had died in Christ's crucifixion.

It is wonderful to see the detail that John captures here. Into the fear of the locked room, the creator again "breathes on them" and they are made alive. This is the breath of *re-generation*. This new life makes them recipients of forgiveness. Not just the forgiveness for wrong and acts of selfishness: Forgiveness for *sin*. Our rebellion can be forgiven and new life received. What a glorious reality!

But notice, after He leaves them they are still behind closed doors for fear of the Jewish leaders. This was a powerful event, but it was not an *empowering* event.

Then the day of Pentecost bursts on the scene -- roaring wind, supernatural fire. Nothing subtle or hidden here.

This event *and only this event* empowered them!

Their fear is gone. They are inflamed with divine motivation to proclaim the risen Jesus to the very leaders who had killed Him and lied about His empty tomb. That flame carried them

---

14 John 20:21-23

15 See Genesis 1:26ff.

to Jerusalem, Judea, and is still driving the disciples of Jesus fearlessly to the ends of the earth.

From this magnificent day, the storm troops of the Good News could not be cowed. They could not be stopped. They are still filling the world with a message of Resurrection, Life and Hope!

Let me tell you....This is really a big deal

PART TWO

The Day Of Pentecost And The Work Of The Church

Introduction to Section II:

As we move forward let me list a few things that are important to remember.

1.   The more distant we conceive God to be, the more we will depend on ritual to communicate with Him. Rituals can be valuable if they *express* an existing relationship. They are useless if we expect them to *establish* that relationship,

2.   To the extent we view God as *only* "out there," the more legalistic our Christian life becomes. We will question his favor and seek to gain it through rules and religion. The more intimate our sense of His presence, the less legalistic and the more natural our faith's walk becomes. The assurance of His approval dramatically increases. Our relationship is not based on seeking His favor but rests in the *fact* of His acceptance. We are now motivated by love, not driven by fear or guilt. We obey because we love Him and are sure of His love for us. Loving obedience defines the expression of our faith.

3.   This confidence of His presence, love and approval is essential if we are to understand our place in the Church described in Section 2.

CHAPTER 7

The Mission of the Church

Let's go back to Jerusalem for a closer look at the remarkable day of Pentecost. This coming of the Holy Spirit upon the followers of Jesus is the center-point of my faith and theology. Everything, from the Garden paradise to the Ascension of Christ, serves to bring us to this day. Furthermore, this day is the launching pad for everything going forward. The God Jesus revealed the God of Abraham, Isaac and Jacob, the Father, places His Spirit in these regenerated believers. The Church is born! Here is the "promise of the Father" Jesus assured them would come.[16]

Suddenly the room is filled with a roar! It sounds like a "mighty rushing wind." There is no dust flying, no leaves blowing. It is not outside -- it is inside. When the shock subsides, they realize, this is *supernatural!* A divine drama has begun.

These people gathered in the upper room had gone to synagogue school. They understood their history and quickly understood the message of the wind. Throughout their Scriptures the God of their fathers was associated with wind. In the events that freed them from Egyptian bondage, Moses stretched his staff over the land and God caused an east wind that brought hoards

---

16 Read Acts 1-3 for the full description of this event.

of locusts (super-grasshoppers). Then reversed it to a west wind and blew them into the Red Sea.[17]

Again, as Israel was fleeing from the Egyptian armies, their flight was blocked by the Red Sea. Moses stretched his staff over the water. Then, the entire nation went back to their tents, presumably to die because the Egyptian army was closing fast. But all night long there blew, "a mighty rushing wind." When they awoke the next morning they saw an escape route right through the sea. They were miraculously saved![18]

When this supernatural sound roared into the Pentecost festival there was no doubt; "the God of our fathers is in the room with us"!

I don't know whether the roaring wind stopped and then the fire came or if the fire appeared during that roar, but suddenly, fire was in the room! It's not clear whether it was a ball or pillar of fire...all we know is there was fire in the room but the room was not on fire. Now that will get your attention! Not only did it get their attention, it re-enforced the fact of God's presence.

They were not terrified in His presence as their ancestors had been. This is the God that Jesus revealed. This is the Father. He is no less awesome and powerful than in the old times. This is the pillar of fire in the wilderness darkness. This is the voice that spoke to Moses from the burning bush. Fire had long been a figure for the presence of their God.

Then, something occurred that none of them could have foreseen. This fiery presence of God began to divide into small flames. These flames came to rest on each of their heads. They now understood that God was not only *out there*--He was not only *with them*--His presence was now *in* them! The flaming swords blocking the entrance to the Garden were now tongues of fire welcoming them home. The circle is complete. His presence is no

---

17 Exodus 10

18 Exodus 14

longer limited to walking with them in the evening. His presence is in them wherever they are. God's presence is now immediate to their everyday experience. This is what Jesus meant when He said, *"I will ask the Father, and he will give you another advocate to help you and be with you forever—the Spirit of truth."* [19]

This new reality began to overwhelm them. Their immediate response was to break into loud and joyous praise to God.

The unexpected wonders of the day continue to unfold. Their praise transcended linguistic barriers. Suddenly, all the people who had crowded Jerusalem for the Pentecost festival heard the glories of this God proclaimed in their native languages! They rushed to the source of all the commotion.

"They are drunk!" (The conclusions of unbelief are often preposterous.) Peter stepped forward to answer their questions. Peter! The most unlikely of the entire apostolic group. This is the Peter who just days before had cowed before the servant girl and denied even knowing Jesus. But, the paralyzing fear is gone. With unprecedented boldness he addresses this mass of astonished people.

Peter reaches 800 years back into Israel's history and quotes a few verses from the little book of Joel. Now, Joel was a prophet who preached only one recorded message. It is about a devastating plague of locusts. The creatures came in clouds of black minions destroying everything in their path.

While speaking at a conference in Western Australia, I referred to this passage in Joel. After the session a rancher came and told me a remarkable story. A few years earlier there had been a horrible infestation of grasshoppers. It lasted for days. He said they came in the evening like a black cloud on the horizon. They literally consumed every living thing. They even stripped the paint off the barns and houses. He described plowing their dead carcasses off the roads like snow. The putrid smell of rotting grasshoppers lasted for weeks.

---

19 John 14:16-17

His story was a graphic illustration of what this Old Testament prophet was talking about. Israel had just gone through the same kind of devastation. The voice of Joel thunders into the stench and destruction with a clear and focused warning, "If you think this plague of locusts is bad, wait until the day of the Lord comes!" (This is the essence of his message.) He then steps off the stage of time, never to return.

Tucked into his message are several verses that had never been understood. They hung suspended and unexplained for centuries. They didn't fit into any of the events of Israel's history. Now, Peter exclaims, *"This is what the prophet Joel was talking about!"* This is where it fits! He begins to quote:

> *"In the last days, God says,*
> *I will pour out my Spirit on all people.*
> *Your sons and daughters will prophesy,*
> *your young men will see visions,*
> *your old men will dream dreams.*
> *Even on my servants, both men and women,*
> *I will pour out my Spirit in those days,*
> *and they will prophesy.*
> *I will show wonders in the heavens above*
> *and signs on the earth below,*
> *blood and fire and billows of smoke.*
> *The sun will be turned to darkness*
> *and the moon to blood*
> *before the coming of the great and glorious day of the Lord.*
> *And everyone who calls*
> *on the name of the Lord will be saved."*[20]

These verses were reserved for the coming of a new age called, "the last days." This Day of Pentecost heralds its dawning. When these things happen, the last days begin. They

20 Acts 2:17-21 (NIV)

are called last days because they are the final stage of God's redemptive intentions for our planet. Humankind can now be told the Good News. We can be forgiven, cleansed and reconciled to God! Instead of impending death, we have the option of everlasting life.

This last age begins at the Pentecost outpouring of the Holy Spirit and it ends with, "The great and glorious day of the Lord." It is a specific window of time with a distinct beginning and distinct ending. There are many theories and books about when this end will come; complicated studies, charts and predicted dates. The fact is, *we don't know*. We aren't supposed to know. It is enough to understand that it is coming. Only God knows when, and He is not telling. We do know this; everything between the opening and closing of this window is of extreme importance. This is a specific piece of time and it has a divine purpose.

During these final days, three things become true that have never existed before. They explain the purpose of the redeemed followers of Jesus throughout this time period.

1. The establishment of a *prophetic community*:
In the last days, God says,
I will pour out my Spirit on all people.
Your sons and daughters will prophesy,
Your young men will see visions,
Your old men will dream dreams.
Even on my servants, both men and women,
I will pour out my Spirit in those days,
and they will prophesy.

Sons, daughters, young men, old men, servants, men and women: This is a comprehensive list including all ages, genders and stations in life. In Israel's history there were many prophets, even schools of the prophets. Occasionally, the spirit of prophecy came upon people as with King Saul. Even Balaam's mule prophesied! Prophecy and prophets are not new. But, to be no longer limited to a specific event or person *is* new. The Spirit of prophecy is available to every member of this believing community at all times.

Also, the role of prophecy has changed. There are no longer exclusive prophets to speak to the people for God. Now there is a prophetic *community* whose very life speaks for God to the on-looking world.

Historically, prophets do three things. They *see* and *hear* and *speak* from God's perspective. They bring God's view to the present moment. This is the new norm for the new community. Young, old, men, women -- all can see and hear and speak from God's perspective. Prophecy is no longer a special gift for select individuals. This is a prophetic community and the immediacy of the presence of God is vibrant in all the details of its life.

2.   The second thing that is true during this age is the world falls apart!

I will show wonders in the heavens above
and signs on the earth below,
blood and fire and billows of smoke.
The sun will be turned to darkness
and the moon to blood
before the coming of
the great and glorious day of the Lord.

These are signals that the world -- the cosmos, is falling apart. Here are the gasps of a dying world order. They do not just suddenly appear at the end of the age. The last days are characterized throughout with these disasters. It is the death process. Calamities happen. Any cursory reading of history reveals this. Disasters, cosmic and personal are a common thread.

Wherever and whenever these occur -- earthquakes, tsunamis, hurricanes, floods, personal tragedies -- they are not sudden outbursts of God's anger. They are indicators that the world is falling apart. These are proofs that we are living in the final stages of our planet's life. The "why" of these horrors is not some hidden mystery that we must explain. We live on a dying planet that is falling apart!

This does not mean we treat the dying world order recklessly or destructively. But, neither are we caught up in trying to "save the planet." Rather, we care for the planet and its environment because it has been created and given to us as a gift from God. Out of love for our Father, we respect it. We cannot stop the dying, but we can care for it in its final days. This is environmentalism in its highest form.

3. The third thing that is true during these "last days" is:

And everyone who calls
on the name of the Lord will be saved.

When do people tend to call on the name of the Lord to be saved? How about when their world is falling apart.

Do you see it? Spirit filled people are the visible presence of Jesus on the planet while it falls apart. Now, this promise of the Spirit was "to all generations, even as many as the Lord our God shall call."[21] That means the Spirit filled, prophetic community is present on the planet *today!* They hear and see from God's perspective and respond to those "calling on the name of the Lord to be saved." These are the *ecclesia* -- the Church; the Body of Christ on earth. The *primary* purpose of the Church is to hear and see and respond to those calling on the Lord.

It's all a great idea but how do we get there? Practically, how does being Jesus in our world work? What, then, is the purpose of our meeting together? How do I move from being a high maintenance religious person to a highly effective Christian, living out the very presence of Christ?

That sounds like a big deal! Let's go there....

---

21 Acts 2:39

CHAPTER 8
The Power Of The Church

But you will receive power
when the Holy Spirit comes on you;
and you will be my witnesses
in Jerusalem,
and in all Judea and Samaria,
and to the ends of the earth."[22]

The birth of the church is a remarkable phenomenon. The shared experience of Pentecost caused Jesus' followers to coalesce into a close fellowship -- a community. Their common faith, the dramatic experience of the Holy Spirit and now their shared purpose served to bind them together as brothers and sisters.

Everything became secondary to this new calling. Even their belongings were no longer considered their own, but were made available willingly to the community. They were people on a mission and everything was focused on that purpose. Their message was clear: "Jesus is alive and well in Jerusalem." The religious leaders' effort to kill Jesus had only succeeded in spreading His powerful influence. Jesus' words were right on. They had indeed

---

22 Acts 1:8 NIV

received power and they were unstoppable in their witness to Him.

The book of Acts has sometimes been called the Acts of the Holy Spirit. It was certainly that. But it is the acts of the Holy Spirit *through the followers of Jesus.* This was not an esoteric move of God apart from human involvement. His action was concretely expressed in the people He redeemed. He does not show up in a sacred ritual or séance. There is nothing secret or clandestine. As Jesus was daily in the Temple teaching; as His miracles were done openly; as His voice was clearly heard; so now his followers met daily in the temple. Their preaching and teaching was public. Their miracles were out there for everyone to see and wonder.

They were neighbors and friends of those who heard them. They were not strangely clad monks pursuing some holy mission. They were common people going about their common life with uncommon power and purpose. They were living proof that Jesus was the Christ and that He was still very much present.

It was left to the Apostle Paul to meld together the teaching of Jesus and the ministry of the Holy Spirit through his followers. His letters are not only commentaries on the life of Christ; they also are the structures that connect Jesus' remarkable years in Palestine with His continuing presence and power through believers. Paul identifies these believers as the Church, the called out ones. This Church he describes as:

"The Body of Christ, the fullness of Him"

Paul came late as a follower of Christ. The audacity of these disciples of Jesus had engendered his hatred. He vowed to put an end to the entire movement. On his way to accomplishing his goal, he was accosted by Jesus Himself and experienced the raw power and awe of His presence. That event transformed his brilliant but misdirected mind and turned it to understand as no one else, the remarkable person...Jesus Christ.

Paul helps us understand what it means to be the Body of Christ on planet earth. He explains her power. He describes her character. He explains how she is to be equipped; how and why she is to gather. He speaks in detail of the methods of her ministry.

The coming of the Holy Spirit on the Day of Pentecost *is the Big Deal*. The cosmic fallout of that big deal ripples forward and defines us as The Body of Christ, The Church, who will be His witness in Jerusalem, Judea, Samaria, to the ends of the earth, indeed, to the end of the age.

When I am talking about the church I am not addressing it as a structure or a beautiful cathedral, ancient or modern. Nor am I referring to its institutions, forms, clergy, rituals or standards. I am not concerned with the forms of something called church. Rather, my focus is the church as a very human expression of God's presence in our world. Jesus did not live, die and return in the Spirit so an *institution* called Christianity could be born. He does not redeem buildings or organizational structures. That we have such things is not particularly sinful and is to some extent inevitable, even needful.

But, we must understand that any structure is to be *vehicular* to a greater purpose. It cannot *become* the purpose. We don't build a beautiful car to simply bask in its beauty. It must be able to take us to our destination or it becomes a museum piece -- look but don't touch. Family vacations would certainly be less exciting if the family sat in a beautiful new van admiring its lines and luxuries, but never left the driveway. It would certainly be safe and less expensive but the van would soon be empty.

Structure is necessary, but it must always emerge out of our passion for mission -- reaching our destination. The vehicle must never become the mission. The vehicle is expendable -- being the presence of Jesus in the world is essential!

If we are to be the active presence of Jesus in our world we must have His power available in a practical form. Jesus made provision for this.

"But you will receive power when the Holy Spirit comes on you..."[23]

---

23 Acts 1:8 NIV

Paul explains what this power looks like in the life of the church. It is important to see that he is describing a force already present; he is not trying to get the power started. He is instructing and correcting, not initiating. He writes so we may better understand, and correctly use, this divine energy in our daily practice.

Now about the gifts of the Spirit, brothers and sisters, I do not want you to be uninformed. You know that when you were pagans, somehow or other you were influenced and led astray to mute idols. Therefore I want you to know that no one who is speaking by the Spirit of God says, "Jesus be cursed," and no one can say, "Jesus is Lord," except by the Holy Spirit.

There are different kinds of gifts, but the same Spirit distributes them. There are different kinds of service, but the same Lord. There are different kinds of working, but in all of them and in everyone it is the same God at work.

Now to each one the manifestation of the Spirit is given for the common good. To one there is given through the Spirit a message of wisdom, to another a message of knowledge by means of the same Spirit, to another faith by the same Spirit, to another gifts of healing by that one Spirit, to another miraculous powers, to another prophecy, to another distinguishing between spirits, to

another speaking in different kinds of
tongues, and to still another the
interpretation of tongues. All these are
the work of one and the same Spirit, and
he distributes them to each one, just as he determines. [24]

It is important to see here that Paul is talking about "spiritual things." The literal word is "spirituals." The term "gift" does not occur until verse 4. This passage is not just about gifts or gifted people. It is about spiritual matters; about how the power of Christ is to be expressed in our world.

Verse 4 begins an explanation of the Divine plan:

There are different kinds of
gifts, but the same Spirit
distributes them.

There are different kinds
of service, but the same
Lord.

There are different kinds
of working, but in all of
them and in everyone it
is the same God at work.

The Holy Spirit gives many different kinds of divine abilities. *The Lord* administrates these distributed gifts -- He oversees and determines their use. *God, the Father* is in charge of the overall working of the operation. He makes sure that everything fits not only the earthly moment, but the eternal purpose as well. This means the Triune God oversees every action of the Body

24 I Corinthians 12:1-11

of Christ! Even the smallest assignment is elevated to eternal proportions.

Paul now gives a remarkable list of some ways the Holy Spirit shows up (manifests Himself) through these Spirit-filled believers:

"Now to each one the manifestation of the Spirit is given for the common good."

There are messages of wisdom and insight.

There are messages involving specific knowledge.

There is supernatural faith.

There are all kinds of healings.

There are remarkable miracles.

There is the prophetic viewpoint of God made clear.

There is the divine ability to understand another's spirit and motive.

There are new languages and even the interpretation of these languages.

What an amazing list! And, it is not exhaustive. The letters of Paul are filled with other ways in which the Holy Spirit shows up in the everyday life of His people, transforming a common event into a supernatural moment.

What is going on here? This is not a hysterical movement designed to continue Jesus' reputation. It is a divine community in which the very Spirit of Jesus lives. It is clear for all to see that the presence and ministry of Jesus is *among us!* This is not a showcase to be observed and wondered at. It is a resident reality that walks into everyday life through the Church, "which is His Body."

Remember, the Church of Jesus, this prophetic community, is on the planet as it falls apart. It is present when people caught in that death plunge, *"call on the name of the Lord to be saved."* There is a message of wisdom that brings insight to their confused, stumbling call for help. There is a knowing word that releases the helpless from the paralysis of indecision. There is faith for the hopeless and healing for the suffering. The miraculous is now probable. God's perspective can be clarified. Motives of those acting against themselves can be disclosed and freedom proclaimed. Even language forms no barrier to the manifestation of the Spirit through the Body of Christ.

The church is walking out the very presence of Christ in their every day circumstances. It touches every appointment, every chance meeting, every conversation, every event of every day, 24/7. It is the "faithful presence" of Christ.[25] It is this faithful presence that penetrates to the core of society and brings redemptive potential to everyone it touches.

To be Pentecostal means that I acknowledge the reality of Christ's immediate and active presence through the Spirit. Spirit baptism is not for decoration or affect, but to enable the Spirit filled believer to *be* Jesus in any situation. We do not relegate the power of the Spirit to an age past or gifted experts in the present. The manifestation of the Spirit is given to *everyone*. There are no limitations imposed.

This understanding allows me to live with the *probability of the miraculous.* We sometimes hear that we must allow for the *possibility* of the miraculous. That means I will be surprised if something supernatural actually happens. But I live with the *probability* of the miraculous. *I am surprised if it doesn't happen!* This is not an arrogant optimism parading as faith, instructing God on what to do, when to do it and how. That is not faith in God. It is faith in faith and it leaves us empty. It blocks us from embracing God's presence at the very time we need Him most.

I must understand that what seems supernatural to me is natural to Him. The miraculous in the life of Jesus flowed naturally.

---

25 James Davidson Hunter develops this wonderful idea in his important book, "To Change the World" Essay III.

This is not surprising. The miraculous is to be expected. The issue is *identity*. If Jesus is the Son of God, God incarnate, then we would be shocked and suspicious if He stood mute before the blind man and gave a word of encouragement to the lepers. Of course He opens blind eyes and casts out demons and walks on water. He is God! We would not expect there to be a grave that could hold Him. Of course He must ascend and transcend this cosmos. He is God! And, if the Spirit of God is truly present in us, isn't the miraculous probable?

"But what if I pray and nothing miraculous happens?" Well, whatever you do, don't blame yourself or someone else. Don't fault your faith or try to manipulate things to look like a miracle happened. *Just be surprised and go on!*

Remember, Jesus was fully man *and* fully *God.* You are not. You are fully man (flawed at best) and filled with His Spirit.

"We have this treasure in jars of clay." [26]

Never underestimate the treasure and never overestimate the vessel! You will never be a Son of God as He was. Live in the realm of probability and leave plenty of room for surprise.

Here then, is the power of the Church. She is emboldened by and empowered with the Holy Spirit. Her power is not used up in building great buildings or establishing great religious institutions. There are buildings (every family needs a house). There are institutions (every endeavor must be organized and administered.) But, these are not her mission. These are but the tools she uses. She is about being the faithful and effective presence of Jesus in the world.

Before we go on, let me talk a little bit about *how* these gifts work. One of the questions I have to ask the 120 speaking on the Day of Pentecost in languages they had never learned is;

---

26 I Corinthians 4:7 NIV

"How did you do that?" Peter, when you preached this incredible Pentecost sermon, really your first one, how did you do that? There is a remarkable spontaneity about the early church after Pentecost. They are in the right place at the right time saying and doing the right things. It is unplanned and unrehearsed. They have a boldness that is astounding.

Peter and John heal the man at the temple gate. (Acts 3)

They answer the rulers who imprisoned them with boldness and clarity with no pre-thought or rehearsal. (Acts 4)

Stephen answers his accusers with such power and accuracy that they execute him. (Acts 7)

Philip, dropped on a desert road in the lap of an Ethiopian official is not stunned by the mode of transportation, but knows exactly what to do and say. (Acts 8)

Don't we have some idea as to their M.O. (modus operandi)? I think we do but we need to look at the way Jesus operated. It seems reasonable to me that if He expected us to continue His ministry in the world He would show us the means of accomplishing that ministry after He was gone.

Jesus told His followers:

"But when they arrest you, do not worry about what to say or how to say it. At that time you will be given what to say." [27]

Of His own ministry, Jesus stated that He said what He heard the Father say and did what He saw the Father doing.[28] This seems to be His m.o., the way He operated.

Fast forward to the Day of Pentecost in Acts chapter 2 and look at a little word imbedded in the story of the disciples speaking in languages they had not learned.

---

27 Matthew 10:19; Mark 11:13

28 See Mark 13:11, John 14 and for further study of this in the early church see also, Ephesians 6 and 1 Peter 4

All of them were filled with the Holy Spirit and began to speak in other tongues as the Spirit enabled them.[29]

The little word "enabled" can also be translated "prompted." They spoke as the Spirit prompted them. A prompter simply tells you what to say or do. Before the days of tele-prompting, the promter sat off-stage and followed every word of the script. When you forgot what to say, he fed you the words and you kept on going.

An actress friend of mine who had been on the Broadway stage for many years told me about their prompter:

"He always said, 'when you don't know what to say next, just keep talking and I will have the words there in plenty of time. Don't panic and don't stop talking'."

That is exactly how all the gifts of the Spirit operate. By the prompting, the nudge, the hunch of the Spirit.

"Say a quiet prayer for that man."

"Greet this girl with a smile."

"Speak to that woman."

"Ask if you can pray for them."

"Help that child."

Haven't you walked away from conversations thinking, "what I said there was really good!"? Don't you remember someone telling you, "What you told me the other day really made an impact on me," and you can't remember what it was? These are all unrehearsed, unplanned and spontaneous. I am not suggesting every crazy thought that wanders through your head is the Holy Spirit. I am saying He uses our natural instincts, thoughts and imagination to prompt us with His words and intentions.

I am intrigued at the fear and resistance to the gift of speaking in tongues. That it has been associated with radical, emotionalized expressions is obvious and regrettable. However, many

---

29 Acts 2:1-4

Christian practices have been radicalized and misunderstood throughout history. Radicalization does not disqualify the gift. It disqualifies the means by which the gift is being exercised.

Speaking in tongues must be de-mystified. In reality, these heavenly languages demand no more emotion than texting on your smart phone. They are not validated by volume, tears, shaking or swooning. Emotionalized, hysterical behavior is not of the Holy Spirit.

We are talking about language, not behavior. We must not confuse the two. When we understand that we are talking about language the conversation becomes much simpler. Paul makes it very clear.[30] Whenever we speak publicly, it has to be understood. So, either talk the local language or have someone on hand to interpret. That makes pretty good sense to me.

He also explains that the Holy Spirit is able to give us a language by which we can speak directly and privately to God.[31] It is a language no man understands so it needs no interpretation. It is spirit to God communication and *He* understands it.

Why is it surprising that God would design a way by which we could communicate directly with Him? His entire plan was a restoration of fellowship. Communication is essential to fellowship and language is unique to God. He invented it and endowed us with the capability to use and understand it. Must we be limited to the micro-sphere of our human linguistic abilities? Language does its job if the hearer understands the speaker. Paul tells us clearly that in this private converse, God not only hears us, He alone understands us. The result is spiritual enrichment. That works for me, and it has for many years.

I think there is a further value implied in this. When we pray privately in tongues, we are following the prompting of the Spirit. It is the same pattern as all the other gifts. It seems to me there is

---

30 1 Corinthians 12

31 1 Corinthians 14

in this a sharpening and a normalizing of our ability to respond to the enablement of the Holy Spirit.

Is speaking in tongues some kind of "magic key" that automatically makes us spiritual? Of course not. There *is* no magic key to spirituality. But I have found that if this gift is included as part of my life of devotion, (not my "devotions") it is a valuable and wonderful vehicle that enriches my communication with my Father and helps me be more alert and bold in my ministry. To me, this is a "big deal."

CHAPTER 9
The Character Of Jesus

Character speaks louder than words and transcends the loftiest actions. Eloquence without character is futile. Ultimately, who you are wins. If the church is to bear a faithful witness to Christ she must wed His power with His character. There was no duplicity in Jesus. He was the same at the dinner table as he appeared to be in the Temple courts. He was "without sin," the Scriptures declare. He did not just speak the truth; He was truth speaking. He didn't just live with integrity, He was integrity lived out for all to see.

"I am the truth..." He proclaimed. It is this Spirit of Truth that indwells the Spirit-filled believer. Truth, honesty, integrity, they are the core of our new man. We have too often witnessed the havoc that a lack of character brings. Whether an evangelist, Hollywood star, politician, sports hero, or local pastor, the fallout is disastrous.

Persons of character are not perfect. They understand that they are flawed. But when those flaws are exposed, they are acknowledged and repented of, not covered up until secrecy can no longer camouflage the ugliness. Position and power may be readily available, but true integrity wins.

King David is a good example. When the prophet confronted him about his sin with Bathsheba[32] he could easily have had the prophet killed and the act hidden. He was, after all, the King. He had the position and all the power. But integrity won. He fell on his face and confessed, "I have sinned before God and man." Power and integrity are wed. The consequences of his horrendous acts of victimization and murder resulted in pain and remorse. However, the intentions of God were served by repentance and both David and Bathsheba were redeemed. After their child of sin died and the tragic results of their action began to bear bitter fruit they gave birth to Solomon who became the great King of Israel and the model of wisdom. [33]

The Church must wed the power of Christ with the character of Christ for the intentions of Jesus to be clearly expressed. Fortunately, this Christ-like character is not left for us to define on our own. Neither are we expected to strive and attain it by our own effort. The character of Jesus is clearly defined in the list of the fruit of the Spirit in Galatians 5:

> *But the fruit of the Spirit is*
> *love, joy, peace, patience,*
> *kindness, goodness, faithfulness,*
> *gentleness and self-control.*
> *Against such things there is no law* [34]

It is important to note that it does not say *fruits* of the Spirit, *plural*. It says the *fruit* of the Spirit, *singular*. These are not nine demands that have to be separately cultivated. It is a picture of the *qualitative* effect of the Holy Spirit's presence. We do not

---

32 The prophet Nathan is an Old Testament type of the Holy Spirit in lives of both Saul and David.

33 See the full story in 2Samuel 11 and 12

34 Galatians 5:22-23 (NIV)

produce these by legalistic, exhausting self-endeavor. If you are filled with the Spirit you have the character of the Spirit. This is what He looks like in you.

I have never heard a cherry tree groaning to produce cherries or an apple tree struggling painfully to yield an apple. However, I see many Christians struggling to produce love, joy or peace and made to feel guilty because their efforts aren't paying off. The very struggle negates them. The greatest advance in Christ-likeness occurs through relaxing in the knowledge of who you are, not in exhausting yourself jumping through self-made or imposed religious hoops.

The key word is, *Relax!* You really are a "new creature in Christ Jesus." You are filled with the Holy Spirit. The qualities of His Spirit are resident in you. Look at this amazing description of who you are, filled with Him.

You are:
Loving
Joyful
Peaceful
Patient
Kind
Good
Faithful
Gentle
Self-controlled

Hello, new person! Would you like to meet your old person? Paul gave that list as well. It is terrible:
Impurity
Debauchery
Idolatry
Witchcraft
Hatred
Discord

Jealousy

Fits of rage

Selfish ambition

Envy

Drunkenness

Orgies

Paul is right when he says these are "obvious."[35] They define the basest motives and coarsest actions of a godless nature. This is the default position of fallenness. It is not that we constantly act this out. Rather, there are no inner boundaries to restrain them. They boil within and spew out when pressure or desire squeezes us. We cannot repress them by our own determination. Nor can we conquer them by endeavoring to release our higher self. The problem is this so called higher self is fallen. We need a *new self*. This is exactly what Jesus provides for us through the Holy Spirit. Paul tells us, "put off the old self…put on the new self." It is this new self that is "created to be like God in true righteousness and holiness."[36]

Preaching that tries to bully us into living righteously then makes us guilty when we fail and flogs us to try harder produces neurotic, self-focused, guilty and bitter individuals. They have to divorce religion from their every day lives to just survive. Our efforts to produce the so-called *fruits* of the Spirit don't even make it for a full seven days. When pressure becomes extreme, they melt into a heap of remorse. Then Sunday comes again. We are reminded of our painful failure and flogged onward. What a pitiful way to live!

---

35 Galatians 5:16-26 NIV

36 Ephesians 4:22-24 You were taught, with regard to your former way of life, to put off your old self, which is being corrupted by its deceitful desires; to be made new in the attitude of your minds; and to put on the new self, created to be like God in true righteousness and holiness.

As a pastor, I am not the least concerned with who you *ought* to be. I am concerned with who you truly *are* in Christ. I want to help you live out this new you! It is natural. It's so natural it is *super*-natural.

Shepherds do not threaten and shame sheep into reproducing and growing wool. That is what healthy sheep do. If they are given a safe and nourishing environment they produce lambs that grow wool and have woolly little lambs themselves. In the same way, you cannot be shamed into the fruit of the Spirit. If you are provided with safety and spiritual nourishment you will evidence the Spirit's presence. It is who you are!

Let's look more closely at the characteristics of this fruit. Since it is part of your new nature, you can choose these qualities rather than act out your old fallen habits. Clear definitions help us put shoes on our faith. I want to define these qualities so they can be more easily recognized and embraced in any given situation.

Love -- Choosing to act for another's highest good

Love in our society (and even in some of our churches) is treated as a feeling. If I don't have a warm fuzzy feeling for someone I don't really love them. But then, if I develop deep feelings and it happens to be another man's wife, there really is nothing I can do. Since I have more emotion about this new person than my wife, I have fallen out of love with my own mate of 30 years and I must now follow my heart. Love is wrapped in my emotions and those emotions drive my decisions. This mislabeling of love produces chaos for individuals and calamities for families.

Agape (the Greek word for love in the New Testament) is not primarily an emotion. It is not a philosophic or abstract idea. Christian love is a verb. It is concrete. It is founded in action.

"God so loved the world that He gave His only son." (John 3:16)

Had He not given, He would not have loved. This is not a statement of His feelings about us. It is a description of His intervention into our death plunge.

The great love chapter of the Bible, 1Corinthians 13, is not a list of feelings, but of actions. It deals with our treatment of one another whatever our emotions may be.[37] It is important to know that you are not shackled to your opinion of, or feelings about, another person. You have the choice to act for that person's highest good.

"But I don't know the highest good in this situation."

You don't have to define love's path. You only need to choose it. "Lord, I choose to act lovingly." He takes it from there and shows you the next right step. It may be small and seemingly insignificant, or it may be daunting and unpleasant, as for example, stepping in front of destructive behavior. Abuse, whether verbal or physical, uncontrolled anger, rebellion, addiction, will destroy the other person's life. To not act against destructive behavior is hatred, not love.

Love cannot just stand by, feel sad and hope. It must act. Godly love may not feel loving to you or the other person. The issue is not your comfort or pleasure, but the other person's highest good. The Holy Spirit in you will define your next move. When He does, move! All you have to do is make the next right choice. Choose to love. When you do, you are choosing up into your true identity. You *are* a loving person. Let your new nature guide you.

Joy -- Living in His presence with gratitude

Always distinguish between *happy* and *joy*. Joy lives deeper than happy.

A young mother in our congregation received the terrible news that her son had been killed in a freak car accident. She was devastated. How do you even begin to deal with such pain? Some

---

37 This concept of love is dealt with more fully in my book, Love, Acceptance and Forgiveness, Regal Press. And my wife's book, Love and It's Counterfeits, Aglow International. Both are available at www. jerrycook.org

time after the memorial service, when the family and friends were gone, we met and I asked, "Tell me, how are you dealing with this horrible loss?"

She looked at me very seriously for a moment then said, "Can I tell you something strange but...good?"

"Of course you can."

She began, "I have never experienced pain so deep and overwhelming. But underneath all that pain and anger, there is something solid that keeps me from utter collapse. I hope you will understand me when I say, it seems like a deep sense of joy. Oh, not joy at my son's death, but a foundational kind of joy that keeps me from completely falling apart and giving up. Does that make any sense to you?"

Immediately I thought of the remarkable scripture, "The joy of the Lord is your strength."[38] I explained to her that Israel's leaders dropped this phrase into the heart of a grieving nation. It is the joy of assurance, of confidence. It is the foundation upon which hope can build. It is the *joy of the Lord*. For her, it was the assurance of His undergirding and unfailing presence at a time of excruciating pain.

Joy is not the result of happy circumstances. It does not arise from an easy day filled with lovely people. Nor is it the willful determination to put on a happy face on a bad day. We are grateful people because the Holy Spirit lives in us and brings with Him, the joy of the Lord. "In your presence is fullness of joy," the Psalmist declared.[39] Because of the indwelling Holy Spirit, we live in the presence of God and therefore in the "fullness of joy." This joy is not an affect of some event. It is the reality of His presence whatever the events may be.

---

38 Nehemiah 8 records the time under Ezra when the Law had been discovered and read to the people. Their deep grief was the realization of their great sin. He encouraged them with these words.

39 Psalm 16:11

As we cultivate the habit of living in the conscious awareness of His presence, gratitude becomes a life-style; a way of seeing. It also becomes a choice. At any moment we can choose joy. We don't have to produce the joy. It is a fact of His presence. We simply acknowledge His joy rather than give in to fear, complaint or anger. The choice releases gratitude. Often we begin to see what was there all the time but hidden by the fog of fear and resentment. Most often, however, we simply become aware of a deep gratitude. It resides below the circumstances, below the painful emotions. It sustains us.

This sense of gratitude is not present only in the chaotic times. It is present *all the time.* It not only holds me together in threatening despair, it enriches and deepens my most delightful moments. Like my little three year old granddaughter, Mya, holding up a huge six inch trout she had just reeled in; Gabriel, my great grandson, running to me with outstretched arms yelling, "Papa! Papa!;" the quietness of a mountain stream at sunset with only the company of caddis flies doing their strange dance above the water; a mother deer with her twin fawns leisurely walking down our lane, with only the furrowed brow of the mountains and the restless ocean observing. This is gratitude residing beneath even the beauty of the moment, this is Joy. This is living life with gratitude.

Because of His resident presence, we bring a grateful person to all of life. Joy neutralizes restless discontent that produces bitterness. Joy deepens every pleasure. Choose the joy of your new self. Gratitude will sustain and guide you.

Peace -- The absence of inner conflict

The peace of the Spirit is not some Nirvana or tranquil state of being. It does not depend on external circumstances or the actions of other people. Peace is not *out there* to be grasped or induced. It is not just hoped for. As with all the fruit of the Spirit, it is *within* you. It describes who you are, the real you, the inside you.

Jesus told His disciples, *"Peace I leave with you, My peace I give to you."* He then goes on to explain, *"Not as the world gives do I give to you. Let not your heart be troubled, neither let it be afraid."*[40] This is remarkable on two counts. It is His peace and is not available from any other source. It is certainly clear that He was not talking about the absence of external conflict. The pressures on Jesus were unrelenting. Rather, He is talking about His total lack of *inner* conflict. His inner peace had to do with His constant communication with the Father and His refusal to live against his Divine values.

We so often lose our inner battles. We may have laudable determination, but we invariably weaken and find that *knowing* what is right is not directly connected with *doing* what is right. We declare ourselves honest, and then compromise. We value friends, but have no time. We declare our marriage and family to have first place, but we are too busy, too tired, too stressed and we end up guilty and angry. Our job dictates. Our appetites entice. Our addictions scream. It is this living against ourselves that threatens our most sacred relationships and destroys us. It pokes holes in our stomach, clogs our arteries and ruptures the blood vessels in our head.

The Holy Spirit ends the war within by delivering the peace of Jesus to our spirit. He brings the values of God's kingdom and writes them on our new heart.

Paul describes it beautifully:

"It is God that works in us to will and to act in order to fulfill His good purpose." [41]

It is not your struggling but God's working that fulfills His purpose and establishes His Kingdom values. This means you can move in one direction inwardly. It's called congruence. The Hebrew word is *Shalom*, which is commonly used as a greeting and a blessing. You can now choose to let go of your inner conflict.

---

40 John 14:27 NIV

41 Philippians 2:13; NIV

Go ahead. Choose into your true identity. That choice will disclose your next right step. You no longer have to make peace happen. You can now bring a peaceful person to the job, the friendship, the marriage. It may not change the circumstances but it certainly changes you as you deal with them.

You are a peaceful person. Step away from anxiety. Announce it, "I choose the Peace of Jesus." It is not a mantra; it is choosing your new nature.

Patience -- Content with God's agenda; at peace with His pace

Patience! The very mention of the word smacks of calamity. We're told, "Don't pray for patience, you're just asking for trouble." It is usually poor old Job that gets the rap. He is blamed for proving that patience and tragedy must go hand in hand.

Actually, Job is not the model of patience in tragedy. He was complaining and arguing all the way. The point of the Book of Job is not patience. The point is to answer the question, "Why do people serve God?" Satan accuses God saying, "The reason people serve you is because you are good to them. Stop blessing them and they will curse you to your face." Job dispels that foolish idea.

"Though He slay me, yet will I serve Him!"[42] Job declares at the height of his suffering, thus silencing Satan's accusation for all time.

Let me liberate you from the idea that the development of patience demands suffering. Granted, tough times can give occasion for patience to be exercised, but they do not, in and of themselves, develop patience. They can just as easily develop bitterness and anger. The choice is yours. That's the great thing! Because of the indwelling of the Holy Spirit and the fruit of His presence you have a choice.

It is important to have a clear and working definition of patience. When I say it is "the choice to be content with God's

---

42 Job 13:15

agenda," I mean several things. First of all, God does have an agenda in your life. Remember, He is working in you. That does not mean He predetermines every event of your life. It means that as you go through your day, He is working for your good. He is participant in the wonderful times as well as the terrible times. He is a great opportunist. He uses the happenings of your day to weave His intention into your life and His intention is always your highest good. He loves you.

Patience discovers the evidence of His presence and embraces His agenda. Be sure you are responding where He is working. Be on the page *with* Him. Don't force Him onto your own page.

The second part of patience is the choice to "be at peace with God's pace." Not only are God's intentions at work but God's timing as well. Solomon wrote in his book of wisdom, *"There is a time for everything."*[43] Timing is important in your spiritual development.

A man came to me and complained,

"I am just not a very good Christian."

"Do you love God?" I asked.

"Yes."

"Are you sure He loves you?"

"Yes."

"Do you ask Him to help and lead you?"

"Yes, all the time."

"When you sin and He points it out, do you stop it and ask His forgiveness?"

"Yes, I try to."

"Well," I concluded, "You are probably about as good a Christian as you can be right now. Relax. Trust His pace and embrace the life He is bringing you."

To be at peace with His pace is not passivity. Rather, it helps us slow down. It relieves the inner struggle and enables us to see

---

43 See, Ecclesiastes 3

where He is working and choose to join Him there. This is the remarkable fruit that the Holy Spirit brings.

Do you see that none of what I am saying is true unless we have been forgiven and cleansed from the tragic effects of our rebellion, and then filled with His Holy Spirit? Do you understand we cannot do any of this on our own? We cannot choose what is not there! But when He enters, His character becomes part of our new man. Now there is a choice, an alternative that has never been available before. When I make that first choice into my new nature, the next right choice presents itself. It's called walking in the Spirit. Not mystical. Not laborious. Not reserved for certain *holy* individuals. It is natural. It is *super-natural!*

Kindness -- Valuing others and treating them with respect

She was the women's dorm mother at our university. It was where Barbara, the beautiful young woman I was dating, lived. We were hopelessly in love (we still are!). We could not stand to say goodnight. Invariably, almost predictably, in spite of our most earnest vows we would miss the curfew. The door of the dorm locked exactly on the minute and we were left to the embarrassment of pushing the doorbell. It rang in Mrs. Hollowell's apartment. She would come and open the door for these two sheepish lovers. You would think the humiliation would cure us. It failed miserably. We were not only hopelessly in love, we were hopelessly late!

Mrs. Hollowell was never mean or cross, but she let us know that she expected better. She managed to be firm but never unkind. She was always gracious even in her role of enforcer of the rules. We were never uncomfortable when we saw her on campus. She always greeted us with cheerfulness and respect.

We were not aware that after our graduation and marriage she kept track of us. She followed Barbara's teaching career and my seminary work. One Sunday, years later, she was in the congregation of the church we pastored in Oregon. She returned often and became a wonderful friend with whom we spent many enjoyable times.

Mrs. Hollowell defines kindness. Far from being a retiring, mousey person, she was a lovely woman of great dignity. Her demeanor was inspiring. She always pulled you upward. She was a living expression of a kind, strong and godly woman.

Kindness does not mean softness. It means kind firmness. It does not need to yell and rant. It is too strong for that. It embraces or resists, but always with the highest respect for the other person. Because we value each other we will deal kindly with one another. This is who we are. It is not something to strive for or struggle with. Whenever you are on the verge of acting harshly and vindictively, take a step back. Let the real you step up. Choose kindness. The Holy Spirit will define its path and lead you.

Goodness -- Living with integrity

Dr. Billy Graham, in speaking to a group of us, stated, "Integrity is being the same person in private as you appear to be in public."

So many times our person is refracted. Its facets differ according to the circumstances and people of the moment. This facet reflects warmth, that one harshness, this one tenderness, that one coarseness and profanity, on and on. We learn to wear hats and play parts to fit the situation. We begin to believe our public introductions and endeavor to live according to other people's expectations. We learn to work the room and please or displease depending on those gathered. We seamlessly slip from one hat to the other.

Goodness knows nothing of an affected persona. A good person is polite and gracious in public and he is equally polite and gracious with his wife and children at home. He doesn't just appear to be honest, he *is* honest. His word is sure and you can depend on it. He is not your friend in public only to make you the object of gossip or ridicule in private. What you see is what you get and what you hear is true.

Goodness does not worry about getting caught. There is nothing to catch. It has no worry of being found out. There is nothing hidden. Of course there is appropriate privacy but if that privacy is suddenly invaded there are no shocking revelations. Goodness does not demand perfection, only honesty. If you are wrong, admit it, seek God's help in repairing any damage then move on.

To live with integrity is to live free from pretense. Image is the default setting in our society. "Image is everything," the ad proclaims. The fact is image may be anything or nothing. The shocking private lives of many of our Hollywood stars, our sports heroes, our politicians and even religious leaders often don't come close to the public image. In fact, it is hardly expected. Rather than being shocked, we simply shake our heads in sardonic non-surprise. Entire industries thrive on disclosing the private lives of public people. But this duplicity is not just Hollywood or music or sports, this is *us*. We are taught to be image builders.

It takes the abilities of the Holy Spirit to break this hold. He is molding us into the "Likeness of Christ" because we were made in the "Image of God." He is not imposing an image on us. He is restoring us to our created intention.

You are a good person not because you *act* right but because you *are* right. Live up into your Goodness. Make the choice and integrity will guide you.

Faithfulness -- Reliable and utterly safe to trust

A tough, grizzled, ex-marine began attending our church with his wife and family. He was a survivor of the brutal and bloody battles of the Pacific during the Second World War. Okinawa, Iwo Jima, Tarawa...these were more than mere Pacific Islands to him. They were memories too horrific to express. They had left scars that were never disclosed. He was a good friend I admired as one of the heroes of my freedom.

One day he came to my office and announced with rare tears in his eyes:

"You are my pastor and I will pray for you and your family every day for the rest of my life."

Now there were tears in both of our eyes as I realized the commitment he was making and knew without a doubt he would keep it.

Years later we resigned that church and moved to Seattle, but I would see Stuart quite often. He adopted a tiny knot of people in a small Washington town on the Columbia River about an hour from Portland. For many years he faithfully drove every week to teach them the Bible and pray for them. He told me how honored he was to be called their Pastor.

Whenever I was close for a conference or other speaking engagement, Stuart would be there. He would tell me two things, "You are still my pastor," and "I pray for you and your family every day." The last time I was with him his mind was clouded and his memory fading but those were still his words to me. He forgot many things and became confused, but he was faithful to his commitment to me and to the little flock he pastored so proudly.

He was faithful to his country, to his God, to his flock and to his friend. He is gone now but there is no doubt that he received the highest commendation from his Commander and Chief, "Well done, good and faithful servant, enter into the joy of your Lord."

What a great picture of faithfulness! This is the person we want to be and try hard to emulate. Unfortunately we are so often disappointed, both in others and ourselves. The flow seems to go the other direction. We hear the appeal of the moment so much louder than the call to faithfulness. "Just do it!" Nike implores. There is no clear understanding of the "it" other than our immediate urge. Our emotions are appealed to in the hundreds of ads we watch on TV. They pop up on our smart phones and computers.

That's part of our society and it is not all bad. It only harms us if our emotions and appetites become commands to act. What is even more harmful is the absence of commitment, whether to a relationship or a promise. Networking demands little loyalty.

The issue of faithfulness is deep but we ask shallow questions. Is it working for *me*? Does it serve *my* felt needs? Will it enhance the bottom line? We apply these questions to our jobs, our friendships and even to our marriages. Utility, convenience, comfort, are fine qualities for the right objects, but they are devastating when they become the values we live by.

There is a societal regression into adolescence. It is a narcissist implosion into "me" and "mine." Self-centeredness becomes the grid through which I determine my actions. Transparency is overlaid with image. Trust is neutralized by compromise. No one in my world is safe, including me. Is ours the first or worst society exhibiting these characteristics? Read history. It is us!

But, I have good news. If you are born again--if you are filled with His Spirit, you have a divine option. These descriptions need not apply to you. You see, the Holy Spirit is called the *faithful* Spirit. God is the *faithful* God. It was said of Jesus that He was *faithful*. It is this quality of faithfulness that is at the core of our new nature. It is not a practiced posture to gain an advantage. It is the genuine article.

Compromise and self-centered motives need not be the default position of your life. You have a new nature. Live up into that identity. Choose to be faithful in whatever circumstances you find yourself.

Let me be clear, *faithfulness does not demand you remain in abusive or destructive situations.* It never goes counter to Love, which always acts for the other's highest good. Love opposes destructive behavior and faithfulness helps define a loving path. That path will always lead you to safety, both for yourself as well as those you love. The Holy Spirit will define that path for you. He will help you see the loving action needed. He will show you what faithfulness to God, and the people in your life, looks like. He will lead you to be faithful to your own new self. He often brings faithful friends you can trust to walk it out with you. I know this, if you will choose into your new nature, you will find it is real and you will see the next right step to take no matter how tiny, or how foreboding and difficult it may be.

Gentleness -- Great strength under control

Gentleness is a great word. If you think it describes a quiet, shy, harmless person, get ready to reboot.

In the Greek language the word is *praus*. It comes from the trainers of ancient Greek warhorses. These were remarkable beasts. They were huge, high-spirited animals that roamed the rugged Grecian hills. The trainer, in great danger and with remarkable skill, would capture and train them. They became some of the greatest warhorses in history. Their strength and courage leaps off the pages of Greek battle lore.

The trainers were a small group and their methods were passed from one generation to another. They never abused or manhandled these great stallions. The horses were far too powerful for that. The method was to learn the animal's language and work with them rather than against them. They achieved incredible results. These enormous animals were so finely tuned that the rider could convey his intent through a certain posture in the saddle, the touch of the toe or heel of his boot, a click of the tongue or even blowing on an ear. These slight movements would trigger a series of military maneuvers. It was enormous power under complete control.

When that degree of perfection was reached, the animal was pronounced *praus*. This is the word translated "meekness" in our English Bibles.

Power without control becomes destructive. The greater the power, the greater the potential for devastation. Big muscles dressed up in bad character and lacking restraint are a sure recipe for disaster. On the other hand, great strength focused and carefully handled can accomplish remarkable feats.

If the Holy Spirit is dwelling in you, you have this quality of meekness. It enables you to maneuver through the chaos and conflict that often surrounds us. You are meek. You have the power of the Holy Spirit and He is training you to focus and use it for God's purposes.

The ancient horse trainer brought his ability to teach the animal to harness its strength and accomplish a great purpose. This is descriptive of the life of the Spirit. He teaches us to manage His power to accomplish God's great purpose. We have the power. We only need learn to sense His slightest touch, to hear His gentle voice and respond confidently to His breath on our heart.

Self Control -- Taking responsibility for one's life and choices

This is at once the most wonderful and the most terrifying of the nine qualities of the Spirit. Wonderful, because it holds the hope of change. Terrible, because there is no one to blame but ourselves for the results of our choices. The person you are is no one's fault or responsibility but your own. Now that is a frightening thought! My mind immediately rebels and comes up with a myriad of reasons to account for my life and situation. Circumstances have forced themselves on me. People have victimized me. "I couldn't help it," is the exclamation of our lives. But, if self-control is actual, I *can* help it.

We must come to grips with the fact that the life we have, good or bad, is the result of our choices. Of course you cannot determine the circumstances that come to you in life, but you can choose who you become as you deal with them. You are not determined by your past or your parentage. You are determined by your choices as you move forward.

I am sorry if your parent was addicted or abusive. That is no shallow or unfeeling statement. The devastation of addiction, alcoholism and abuse on children is horrific. The pain cannot be imagined nor the confusion comprehended by anyone who has not experienced it.

I was never abused. My parents drank nothing stronger than root beer. I do not understand the inner turmoil and torture of those so damaged. However, I can say to you, though we are dramatically *influenced* by our past and the people in it, our past does not *determine* us.

My good family did not determine my future but it certainly influenced the decisions I made. Our present is not merely the sum of our history. It is the sum of the choices we made as we lived out that history.

I cannot predict or change the behavior of others. I cannot always control the circumstances. If my life depends on things that can't be changed, on things beyond my ability to control, I am without hope. I'm adrift on a sea of unmanageable currents and unpredictable storms. To search for someone or something to blame is futile. If you are the cause and I am the result, then I am hopelessly fixed. I am imprisoned to your action.

On the other hand, if I am separate from your opinion and can step aside, hear or watch you and then choose an appropriate response, I am free. If I can experience the circumstances but not be consumed by them; if I refuse to let them choose for me but rather choose the best action to take myself, I am free. I am free to make the decision and I am free to live with the results of that choice. If I can uncouple my person from the events of my past and choose my present and future path, I am free.

But who is this self we are liberating? Isn't that the crucial question? If it is the same old self, it will walk back into the same old prison of blame and be welcomed by the old cellmate, Hopelessness. You dare not give control to the old self!

But, what if there is a new self? What if there is a "new creature in Christ Jesus," and new birth is a reality? Then everything changes and you can be assured that the "old things are passing away; all things are becoming new."[44] For the first time you can begin to make right choices and take responsibility for the results. You can even take responsibility for a wrong or foolish choice and when you do, the Holy Spirit will faithfully guide you through its effects. We are new persons with clear identity. We can see ourselves separate from the opinions of others and not victims to the stuff of our lives.

Of course other people's opinions matter, but I am not the sum total of their opinion. I bring a defined person to these opinions and evaluate them accordingly. I observe my circumstances and make a clear choice regarding them. They may have imposed themselves on me, but I will take charge of who I become as a result of their imposition.

This is not some arrogant, "I'm the master of my fate," idea. It is the result of the inner presence of the Holy Spirit. He shows me the next right choice no matter how wrong the last one may have been. By a series of right options, which I now have the power to choose, He leads me into His health and intention for my life. Because He is healing my brokenness I am able to be a healer rather than a victimized complainer.

There is a remarkable promise recorded in the book of Deuteronomy given to Israel by God when they were facing their enemy:

"The Lord himself goes before you and will be with you; he will never leave you nor forsake you. Do not be afraid; do not be discouraged."[45]

Now, this wonderful promise is internalized. It is a fact of every moment of our day. It is the Spirit of this powerful God who indwells us. His presence frees us from the fear of opinion. His presence releases us from victimization. His presence brings a divine, redemptive option to every intersection of our life.

---

44 1 Corinthians 5:17 "Therefore, if anyone is in Christ, the new creation has come: The old has gone, the new is here"

45 Deuteronomy 31:8 (NIV)

Don't look for some external voice or sign. It is the voice of His Spirit *within*. Hearing and responding to this inner voice is now natural. This new nature can be trusted with self-control.

As we end this section, let me make a few summary observations.

We live in a society in which external boundaries are being erased and internal boundaries are collapsing. We are left to chance and chance leaves us hopeless. There is nothing we can do, so it doesn't matter what we do. Good luck!

No! Good News! There is an old self to take off and a new self to put on.[46] This new self has the nine qualities we have just discussed in the fiber of its character.

Now, there is something very important here. If you are not born again, if His Spirit does not live within you, nothing I have said is true for you. My suggestions about choosing will not work for you over the long run. In fact, they will only discourage you. This is not a list of self-help principles to strive for. It is a picture of the qualities the Holy Spirit brings when He enters your life.

Remember, we have emphasized how important it is to make the *next right decision*. Perhaps your next right choice is to invite Jesus to give you new birth and fill you with His Spirit. Personally enter into the power of the Resurrection. Experience for yourself the pure energy of Pentecost. Ask Him to change your family of origin. Become a child of God. It is as easy as praying, "Jesus come into my life and fill me with your Presence."

---

46 Ephesians 4; Colossians 3 (NIV)

CHAPTER 10
Equipping The Church

We have discussed the Mission, Power and Character of the church. It is important that these be laced together seamlessly so the Church can function naturally and effectively. The means for achieving this is found in Ephesians 4.

This is why it says,
"When he ascended on high,
he took many captives and gave gifts to his people."

(What does "he ascended" mean except that he also descended to the lower, earthly regions? He who descended is the very one who ascended higher than all the heavens, in order to fill the whole universe.)

So Christ himself gave the apostles, the prophets, the evangelists, the pastors and teachers, to equip his people for works of service, so that the body of Christ may be built up until we all reach unity in the faith and in the knowledge of the Son of God and become mature, attaining to the whole measure of the fullness of Christ.[47]

---

47 Ephesians 4:7-13 NIV

In this remarkable passage, Paul established that in Christ's descent to this "lower earthly region" (planet earth), He liberated man to not only be participants *in grace*, but to be distributers *of grace*. Grace and gifts are joined. The ability to continue Christ's gifts of grace is given to this freed man and then Christ extends His presence "to fill the whole universe." It is a Christ-infused universe. He is present. Now we have the choice of relationship with Him.

He gives five gifts to the church "to equip God's people for works of service." The result of these gifts is a church fully prepared to minister as the Body of Christ in the world. But the effects of a ministering church are felt not only in society at large. There are dramatic results *within* the church community as well. The church becomes strong, united, mature, and attains the "full stature of Christ." It begins to look and act like Christ.

This is an incredible concept. Remember, Jesus has ascended and His presence fills the whole universe. That means He is present but invisible. He no longer has an earthly body that we can relate to. The Church becomes His earthly body. She is given His Spirit, His power, His character and now these five gifts specifically to prepare her to make Him visible. That is what a body does. Your body gives you visibility and allows you to express yourself. The Church is Christ's body and gives Him visibility and expression in our world.

These five vital gifts of Christ to the church are:

"Some apostles,"

"Some prophets,"

"Some evangelists,"

"Some pastors and teachers."

These have been exhaustively discussed. We have done everything from ignoring them altogether, to making them an ambient influence, to ordaining them as official positions in the church hierarchy. Because of this confusion, the church has experienced enormous damage and the crucial results these gifts were given to achieve are neutralized.

The "what" and "how" has been debated but not so much the "why" of these. Let me raise three why questions. I am sure there are many more but these relate directly to our present conversation.

1. Why would He give these after "He ascended...to fill the whole universe"? (Ephesians 4:10)
2. Why these particular gifts?
3. Why give them to the Church?

As to the first; I understand this reference to descending and ascending to refer to the period of His incarnation on the earth *("lower regions of the earth")* and his ascension from the earth *("in order to fill the whole universe").* He came; He liberated; He ascended to His place of exaltation and universal presence. Because He became present universally, He became invisible locally. Invisibility does not in any way denote absence. It simply means there is no physical body that can be touched or seen.

The day of Pentecost birthed the Church and made the *expressed presence* of Jesus universally available on earth through Holy Spirit infused believers. We now have, "The Church which is His Body, the fullness of Him..." But the statement, the ideal, is not the actual. How does this group of Spirit-filled believers actually become "The Body of Christ"? I know I have introduced a "how" question, but we must understand that we are dealing here with both a reality and a process. This is common to our faith.

We are saved, yet we are being saved

We are perfect, yet we are being perfected

The Kingdom of God is now and in the process of coming So it is here. We are the Body of Christ, yet we are becoming like Him.

This brings me to the second question: Why these gifts? These gifts describe His ministry. He was indeed the sent one. That is the definition of apostle; one sent with a specific mission and message. He was a prophet, evangelist, pastor and teacher. These encompass His ministry. His body must have His power (gifts of the Spirit); His character (fruit of the Spirit); and it must also express His ministry. Thus, these five things that comprise His ministry are given as gifts to the church, "to equip his people for works of service." Or, as another version puts it, "for the equipping of the saints for the work of the ministry." (NKV)

This focuses the third question: Why are these gifts given to the church? In this Ephesians 4 section it is clear that these gifts are not only given so the church can replicate the ministry of Jesus, but in the accomplishing of that ministry they experience unity, maturity and come to fully look exactly like Jesus. By ministering apostolically, prophetically, evangelistically, pastorally and instructively we "attain the whole measure of the fullness of Christ." In other words, Jesus becomes visible and we become "His witnesses" as He predicted we would.[48]

Christians have sought Christ-likeness in every conceivable place except the only place it is available, namely, through ministering the way Jesus did. All our study, our meditating, our preaching and religious practice are not ends in themselves, they are means; they are vehicles. They inform and sharpen our ministry in order that we may grow. If all our religious activity does not lead to this ultimate ministry purpose, we are simply well informed and highly disciplined religious people.

Thus, the equipping gifts. Let's look at them more closely. If they are important enough for Jesus to give as gifts to the church, we must understand them and make sure they are functional in our church community.

Note that these gifts are not written with capital letters in this scripture. It is apostle, not Apostle. It is prophets, not Prophets, etc.

---

48 See Acts 1:8 ff.

We must see it. Jesus did not give five *experts* to the Church to do all the ministering. He gave five *gifts* to the Church so that His grace can continue to be concretely expressed in this world through all believers. These are not designed to work independently as though each just goes about his prophesying, evangelizing, etc. with no regard to the other or to the church community at large. It seems clear to me that these are given so the church as a community can be apostolic, prophetic, evangelistic, pastoral and instructive.

These are not people floating over the globe doing their thing. These are five gifts of grace Jesus intends for His Body so that He can be made visible in the world – in the community of faith and in the daily life of every believer. Whenever, and wherever, this Church gathers she must be gaining more apostolic, prophetic, evangelistic, pastoral, and teaching expertise so that when she explodes into the society Jesus is present and visible.

Let's look at these more specifically.

Apostles

"And He gave some to be apostles."

When apostles function within the local church community whatever size, whatever brand, they help that local community be apostolic. What do I mean by that?

The place we usually go for an understanding of this gift is to the twelve Apostles and the Book of Acts. It is interesting that the majority of the Twelve are not mentioned in Acts. Peter and John are. James became the head of the church in Jerusalem. John drops out and Peter takes predominance. Then, Peter fades and it becomes primarily the Acts of Paul. There is historical evidence that some of the remaining eight were responsible for establishing Christian beachheads in other nations, but these are not mentioned in the book of Acts. It is safe to speculate that some of them left Jerusalem with the multitude of other Christians when the persecution was fired by Stephen's death. Likely they were part of the resulting spread of the Gospel but their path is not followed. The four that are followed were responsible for blowing holes in the religious and pagan/secular cultures and planting the Gospel.

It is this forward and relentlessly outward momentum that apostolic influence drives. It forces us out of our buildings and off our porches. It pushes us into our neighborhood, community, city, state and world. An apostolic church cannot sit still. It has spiritual A.D.D. But it is not just energetic or frenetic. It is focused, purposeful and laser targeted. How does it get that way and stay that way? Jesus has given apostles to the church and they won't let us rest.

We have been so busy trying to figure out who these apostles are and what they do that we have neutralized the entire concept and reduced its force to discussion groups.

"They are missionaries."

"They are Bishops."

"They are successful pastors."

The debate goes on. Granted, some missionaries are apostolic, some bishops and pastors may be. But to reduce this gift to a position is to miss the point and forfeit the power. We have looked for "Apostles" and missed the apostles of the local church community.

Phil and Jan, a young couple in our congregation, came to my office one day. They believed they were called to Vietnam as missionaries. Our congregation was large and I didn't know this couple well.

"Great," I said. "Let's start right away. You only have to drive ten miles into the center of our city." I explained there was a huge complex of high-rise apartment buildings exclusively inhabited by Vietnamese families.

Phil and Jan took an apartment in the middle of that "little Vietnam." They lived in isolation and suspicion for a year. During that time they did manage to learn the predominant language and became able to communicate reasonably well but they were shunned and insulted as intruders in the apartment community. Our church family was aware of what they were doing. We prayed, but frankly, were very concerned for their well-being. They were working and supporting themselves, but the little apartment in middle of that hostile community was their only home.

One night, they heard loud crying and screaming coming from the apartment next to them. They ran to the open door not knowing what to expect. They found a young woman in the throes of a complicated and painful childbirth. Jan was a pediatrics nurse. (Coincidence?) She took control of the situation, calmed the terrified family and assisted that young mother to the successful birth of a healthy little girl.

As the story spread through the complex the racial and social barriers crumbled. There is not enough space to tell you all the stories, but over time there emerged a strong Christian community which spread through that complex and into the Vietnamese community of our city.

That is apostolic. Phil and Jan were some apostles Jesus had gifted us with. There were many more of our apostles who broke through the prostitution and human trafficking barriers; spearheaded the rescue of hundreds of Cambodian boat people; successfully broke through political and educational walls. They invaded office buildings and businesses, planting the Gospel. These were apostles. You will never hear their names and I don't even know all of them or their stories. They were certainly not authorized from my office. But I can assure you; Jesus set some in that church to be apostles and they injected the entire church with their fervor. They forced us forward and outward and made "impossible" a meaningless term.

Who are your apostles? You will recognize them, not because they are dramatic but because they are poking holes in the pagan society and opening new streams for the ministry of Jesus. We will never understand a broader application of the apostolic until we give place to the local apostles Jesus has set in our congregations. Please. Don't tag them as apostles! Don't give them a label. They are ministering naturally because Jesus has set them in the church. You do not need to specify them; you need only define what apostle means in your setting and tell stories that illustrate your point. Pastor them. Don't mess with their gift. Help them steward it. Give them a loving and supportive context. Theirs is only one of the five. Apostles need the other four as much as anyone else. They must be in the mix of congregational life.

Prophets

"And He gave some to be prophets."

Perhaps the most maligned of these five gifts is the prophet. There are roving prophets giving "words" to people and demanding church congregations give them a platform. Others stand and "prophesy" in the congregational gathering often expounding things that take neither a gift nor a prophet to know. It seems like the worst thing to do is put the title "Prophet" on somebody. The temptation for them is to try and be one. The temptation for us is to make them prove it.

I do know this; there are people who have remarkable insight into what Jesus is doing and saying. They often convey their insight in casual conversations. Without trying to be profound they make a remark or give a viewpoint that opens an entirely new understanding. It can at times be more specific or something they want to express to a specific person and even a group. But they are not acting officially. They are simply and naturally going about their life prophetically.

During a conversation in my office, Tom mentioned how much he liked talking with Steve. When I asked why, he said, "He just says stuff that helps me understand God's ways better." I had heard that same thing about Steve several times. I didn't appoint him as the church prophet. I just noticed him and observed how often he was in conversations that ended in a short prayer and a kind hug. I sought him out and told him I had observed his quiet influence and thanked him for being so sensitive to people. I asked him if he would mind if once in a while I suggested someone connect with him or perhaps introduce him to someone I wanted him to meet. He agreed to my request and his prophetic life influenced many in our community.

In a congregation of several thousand I had a whole lot of Steves and Sallys and Ralphs in my pocket. They were men and women of all ages, sizes and shapes. None of them looked particularly "prophetic." Jesus had set them in the church as prophets. They constantly reminded us that Jesus Christ's voice and understanding was in this place. They quickened our ears to the voice of the Spirit.

This prophetic gift can be expressed in a number of different ways. John came to me before one of our morning services and said, "I think the Lord wants us to have a special prayer for sick people today." I asked, "Any special sickness or conditions?" He answered, "No, just a specific time to pray for the sick."

"Would you be willing to come to the front and say the prayer?"

"Yes, I'll be happy to."

We didn't have a prayer line and I laid hands on no one. Neither did John. At an appropriate time I told the congregation that Jesus was especially present today to heal the sick. I asked those who wanted a healing prayer to stand. People stood all over the building. We then had people seated nearby join them and extend their hands while we prayed. I asked John to come and pray. He prayed a simple prayer asking Jesus to confirm His desire to heal the sick. I then invited those who had experienced healing to raise their hands and we collectively thanked Jesus. The stories of miraculous healings went on for weeks.

We learned several things that morning. We learned the value of the prophet. And, because the prophet was faithful, we learned that Jesus could do the miraculous through each of us. Great lessons!

My point is that it all took place because Jesus had given some prophets to the church. We didn't wait for someone to suddenly feel prophetic and disrupt the service. We knew our prophets. They were us. Sometimes, during our public services they would quietly go to one of the other pastors or designated people and mention something the Lord had shared with them. If appropriate, whoever was leading the service was alerted and determined when and how it would be brought to the congregation. It was neither distracting nor dramatic.

Because of these prophets, God's viewpoint was clear and the spirit of prophecy thrived. People became aware that Jesus speaks to people just like us. You don't have to be an expert. The gathering of the Body of Christ gives visibility to the prophetic and increases our ability both individually and as a faith community to hear and respond to the voice of God wherever we are.

Evangelists

"And He gave some to be evangelists."

I'm including these little scenarios from our church to illustrate ways in which these gifts can be sanely expressed in a local community of faith. They are not intended to be normative, simply illustrative. I hope they exemplify how we can express our gifts naturally and with dignity in the public gatherings of our church family. It is essential that we establish ways to do this. It is vital to the accomplishment of Christ's ministry and therefore to our growth into Christ-likeness.

Because we had many visitors and were a large group, the person leading the service would often ask the congregation to turn to those near them and get acquainted. If the person was new, they were welcomed and possible friendships could be seeded. The leader would usually say something like; "If you have some extra room at your lunch table or if you are going out to eat after the service, invite someone to join you." It was amazing the stories this generated. One thing we knew for sure; the evangelists would be all over it.

Our evangelists were not formally trained to jump you and start you down the road of some planned sales technique. We knew who the evangelists were because time after time we heard the stories from their lunch or dinner tables of the people who had come to Jesus. There were a lot more stories we never heard, but they were out there. Evangelists!

I noticed there were people who always seemed to have someone with them; a fellow-worker, a neighbor, someone they met in a restaurant or a pub. They were like flypaper – people stuck to them. They would introduce me to Mary or Sam or Sue, "They are just beginning to follow Jesus," or, "This is the first church they have ever gone to;" something that would let me know evangelism was alive and well. Jesus had indeed given "some evangelists." Because of them, evangelism was a given in the church life.

Stories are so important. We must develop vehicles for their telling and hearing. Jo Barrett volunteered to publish a four-page newspaper for our congregation called, <u>Family Matters.</u> It came out each month primarily for the purpose of telling the stories of our church community. She would interview new people and families, detail recent events and note future ones. She always had a poignant human-interest story. The experiences of new believers were often included.

The message was clear. Evangelism wasn't a committee nor were evangelists specialists called in to teach techniques. They were "us." They were not designated as such. They wore no badge. But, in our relationship with them we were motivated to be open for business because Jesus really is "seeking and saving the lost," and He is doing it through us.

There is certainly a place for the gift of evangelist in the broader Christian community. But their purpose is to "equip the saints for the work of the ministry," not to do the saints' work for them.

Pastors and Teachers

"And He gave some to be pastors and teachers."

Jesus was the "Good Shepherd." We expect His Body to express His love and care for the sheep, even the lost sheep.

The term pastor has been formalized. We think of it as a positional, religious occupation. Of course there must be leaders in church communities. Jesus clearly calls specific people to that vocation. I happen to be one of them. The problem is that the idea of position over-powers our thinking. We forget that the *church family* is called to be a good shepherd; a pastor to one another and to the world outside.

A pastor is primarily one who cares. The church, as the Body of Christ, makes Jesus visible as it cares. It cares for the lost, for the found, the weak, the strong, the hungry, the glutton, the poor, the rich, the nice and the obnoxious. The church is the visible heart of the Good Shepherd. Pastors understand they will never meet a person for whom Jesus did not die; a person for whom He does not care.

Mark and JoAnn bought a used funeral home limo; big, long, black and shiny. Every Saturday night they put hot coffee and some sandwiches in the back and headed for the inner city. They would go to the districts known for rampant prostitution and pull their big car up to the curb. JoAnn would motion to one or perhaps two of the girls. She would tell them immediately that they didn't want their services. She assured them they would get paid but wondered if they would like a short break and a cup of coffee. As you'd expect, she was met with a lot of suspicion and their offer was not always accepted. But those who took the offer of a sandwich a short ride and rest experienced the visible Jesus caring for them.

Mark and JoAnn were not official. I didn't know this Saturday adventure was going on until someone told me and I verified the fantastic story with them. Many of those girls found Christ and were able to begin the long, difficult and often dangerous road out of their street life. But this was not primarily an evangelistic mission. Evangelism was serendipity of a caring mission.

Theirs is an exceptional story. Most were not. There were many pastors all through the congregation. They were all ages, boys, girls, men women, couples, former gays...they all led the way and because of them we were known as a church that cared.

Caring did not happen only "out there." We wanted a pastoral community with a minimum of programs. It is necessary to leave people time to look and listen for needs and to meet them in Jesus' name.

I was recently speaking in a church where many of the people were out of work and struggling. The church found an outlet that gave them bread, pastries, potatoes and fruit. It was stacked on tables in the lobby for anyone to take. The congregation was encouraged to take some for themselves and a little extra to give to anyone needing it.

A church must be a caring community and it is the pastors who are given as gifts to help us understand how to care and to drive us away from our self-centeredness. The Pastor must make sure the pastors in our congregations are pastored and their caring gift valued. They are indispensible to equipping the saints for the ministry of the church.

Often the roles of pastor and teacher are combined into pastor/teacher. This passage certainly allows for that. I separate them because in my experience I have met those who seem uniquely gifted to make very complex things simple. They seem to be able to grasp a concept and translate it vividly and we say, "I see that," "I can do that," "Now that makes sense." They explain things. Whatever they are doing whether working on their car, cooking, fishing or leading a home study, they are explaining and teaching. They are not obnoxious know-it-alls. They just get it and can explain it.

I hear comments like, "Phil and I were talking about the sermon and he explained one of the things you said. He helped me understand," or, "Ann and I are meeting for lunch on Wednesday and we are reading the Bible together. She helps me understand what the author is trying to say."

I know the teachers are at work. Some teach formally, most do not but they all help us understand what being Christian is all about. They explain it. They sponsor conversations. Their insight spreads to the church community and penetrates into our everyday life. They are equipping the church to do the work of the ministry.

Here's how these all work together.

Jesus' power (Romans 12) plus Jesus' character (Galatians 5) plus Jesus' equipping (Ephesians 4) equals: The visible presence of Jesus in our faith community, in our everyday life and in our world. Jesus now has a body. He can be seen, felt, experienced, trusted and believed in.

The Church has largely failed here. People cannot accept or reject Jesus unless they see and experience Him. But, He has been kept invisible. Instead, He's acknowledged once or twice a week when we meet in a cathedral, a warehouse or an apartment. He is then left there like a disembodied spirit until we decide to come back to "God's house" and meet with Him again. The rest of the time He hovers around, blessing our meals and keeping us safe when we drive. Mostly, He's just on call for us and mad at sinners.

Many times people aren't rejecting Jesus. They are rejecting a caricature because the church has failed to give Him visibility. He must have a real, flesh and blood body. He may still be rejected but at least it is actually Him, not a religious distortion that is being rejected.

This matter of Pentecost; of being filled with the Spirit; of using the power and living out the character of Jesus; of being in a community that is apostolic, prophetic, evangelistic, pastoral and instructional; one equipped to be "the whole measure of the fullness of Christ" in the world. That is a Big Deal!

CHAPTER 11

The Gathered Church

Who is this Gathered Church? To this point I have focused on individuals and their ministry in the Body of Christ. They are filled with the Holy Spirit of God. They have available all the gifts of the Spirit. They are the living fruit of the Spirit. They are equipped and bringing Jesus to their world. What a power-packed bunch of people are gathered here!

Jesus said where there are two or three people gathered in His name He is present. Can you imagine the intensity of His presence when a large group of Spirit filled people is together "in His name"? They are not coming as defeated sinners who have made it through another exhausting week. They are not here out of a legalistic demand motivated by guilt and fear. They are the "living stones" of God's temple.[49] They are the individual expressions of Jesus' presence in their work, their neighborhood, their social and business relationships. They have made Jesus visible in every strata of the city's life. They have been standing in the path of Satan and his parade of demons as they tried to bring death and destruction. They have resisted and stood their ground. They have loved the poor and cared for the broken and

---

49 1Peter 2:5

hurting around them. This is a powerful group of people! *They are the ministering staff of the church.*

However, not only do they bring their power, they also bring their humanity. This remarkable treasure of God's Spirit is contained in "earthen vessels."[50] We are not only powerful. We are "earthy." This does not mean we are overt sinners, but we do need forgiveness for our sins. It means we experience the tiredness, weakness and sickness of the human condition. We face the heartache, discouragement, frustration and emotional pain that are part of living in a fallen world. When we gather, we need to be encouraged, strengthened and healed.

When we gather together we are safe. We don't have to pretend we are perfect, victorious and spiritual. We can cry here. We can confess here. We can be healed here. We are with brothers and sisters who are holy and earthy just like we are. We don't have to impress others or defend ourselves. We freely lift our hands in praise and are joined by a host of other worshippers. Worship is not just my voice, my heart, my spirit. It is *our* voice, *our* heart, *our* spirit. We are members of one another and when we are gathered our brotherhood is intensified.[51] Our spirit breathes, "I am not alone".

Jesus is visible when we meet. He is visible in our prayers and our singing. He is seen as we experience His healing life and learn from His word. In his letter of 1John, the Apostle makes a remarkable statement.

"No one has ever seen God. But if we love each other, God lives in us, and his love is brought to full expression in us."[52]

In other words, God looks like His people loving one another.

---

50 2Corinthians 4:77 But we have this treasure in earthen vessels, that the excellency of the power may be of God, and not of us. (KJV)

51 Romans 12:5; Ephesians 4:25 (KJV)

52 1John 4:12 (NLT)

As this Church gathers, the inroads of self-worship and the idolatry of individualism that a secular society presses on us are exposed and cleansed. Men and women, specifically called by God teach us from His Word. This anointed teaching and preaching is a form of prophecy and gives us God's perspective. It illuminates His will and ways. Our appetite for His Word is both satisfied and increased.

And, we "hang out." We have a cup of coffee and share stories; we laugh and enjoy one another. This fellowship makes Jesus visible.

Does this all sound hopelessly idealistic? I hope not, but I'm afraid it might. The problem with the gathered church is *us*. *We* are imperfect and that is intensified when we earthen vessels (Literally: clay pots) get together. We have wrongly tried to solve this by endowing certain leaders among us with less "clay-potishness" than others. These we call the "clergy." They do the worship in front of us. They minister to us. They listen to us, come to us, serve us, pray for us, marry us, bury us and go around the world as our missionaries. They are holy and we are scandalized when they don't live up to our lofty standards of spirituality.

We do pay them for their services. And, we come to watch them perform their duties and tell us how to improve our attitude, be successful in our business and families and how to quit sinning so much. We are even entertained by a worship band often complete with smoke and lights. Then we are dismissed to go back to our secular life in "the world."

"Well," you declare, "What a cynical and exaggerated picture."

You are right, of course. But what is not exaggerated is the ominous canyon we have created between our church life and our everyday living. Unfortunately, going to a church or small group meeting during the week does not bridge it.[53]

---

53 For a full discussion of this point, see my book; *Monday Morning Church*: Schuster Books. You can order it from my web site, www.

There must be seamlessness to our Christian faith in order for us to make sense of it and for a pagan world to make sense of us. It is this seamlessness that is served when we gather as the Church. In this brotherhood, this community of faith, we are pressed to be truly spiritual. To love God and be equipped to "love our neighbor as our self" is not accomplished by any legalistic discipline imposed from without. It is the result of meeting the challenge of being part of an authentic and loving community.

Just as there is no mythical sacred/secular dichotomy, there must be no clergy/laity fracture. There are leaders, of course, but they are not hierarchically arranged in harsh positions. They are distinguished by role but not by power. Jesus said plainly, *"It will not be with you as it is with the Gentiles who rule over you."*[54] The only allowable relationship between us is that of a servant. I am free to serve you. I am not free to "boss" you.

This is nearly impossible for us to grasp because most of our positions of order are vertical; powered from the top down. Sadly, even our marriages and parenting roles are often treated as positions of power. It is no wonder that when we come to the gathering of the church we automatically structure ourselves in power layers. We construct positions, endow them with job descriptions and choose the best employees to fill them. Very often, even the job description bows to power and the position continues long after the job is outdated.

In the Body of Christ, the greatest power is not position, but relationship. We are not bound together by structure; we are bound together by love for one another and any structure we develop must reflect and enhance this bond. In this loving community, serving one another is made orderly by our mutual care for and our recognition of the particular gifts of each person making up this Body. Paul makes clear in his writing that no gift is

jerrycook.org or from your bookseller.

54 Mark 10:42-44 NIV

greater than any other. They are equally important however visible or hidden they may be. This gathered church is one Body and it ministers to itself in love. [55]

Because of our theology of Pentecost, we understand that as we gather there is the *real* presence of God. He is present in all of life, but when we gather "in His Name," the presence of God is intensified. It is a time when we not only hear His voice individually; we hear His voice to us collectively.

Pentecostalism has too often expressed this intensity in a loud, emotional and demonstrative style, which embarrasses the regulars and terrifies the visitors. It has confined it to a "message in tongues," and hopefully, an interpretation or some "word of prophecy." Because these can erupt at any moment, we tend to outlaw them, confine them to small controllable groups or simply leave no time of silence in the meeting where they might spring up.

To have a theology of Pentecost has nothing to do with a certain public style. It does not demand volume, sweat or emotional exertion. The enduring point of the Day of Pentecost was not its emotion or its volume (though it had plenty of both). It was the infusion of believers with the Holy Spirit of God. The first effect was communication. Every one on the road outside heard these people praising and glorifying God in their own native languages. It was not just emotional noise. These disciples were transformed from a fearful group behind closed doors to a dynamic community that exploded in love and power. The quake of Pentecost started a tsunami that is still engulfing the world.

Traditional Pentecostalism has often made the mistake of wanting the event of Pentecost to happen again as in the book of Acts. It prays and waits for the fire to fall and speaking in tongues to sweep over it again as "in the beginning." By focusing on the experience, the larger point of the Spirit's coming is often

---

55 1Cor. 12:12-26 NIV

missed. The Holy Spirit has been given to the church and that event does not need to be repeated any more than the Incarnation of Jesus needs to be repeated historically. Their effect eternally transforms reality. We do not have to "tarry" for the Holy Spirit. We do not need to beg Him to come or negotiate with Him. He is here! We only have to receive Him.

However, just as regeneration must be individually received, so also, the baptism of the Holy Spirit must be individually received. As the regenerated person experiences evidence of his new birth, so also the Spirit-baptized person experiences evidence of the Spirit's infusion. The gifts of Jesus' power are now evident and a more spontaneous and bold response to the Spirit's direction is clear.

The Holy Spirit allows this God-infused universe to become personal. It is not a philosophical idea about the cosmos. I know this is a God-infused universe because I am a Spirit-infused person…a Spirit-baptized person. This baptism is not just an academic or mental assent to His presence. It is received by faith, but that faith brings me into a new experience of transformation. It is not salvation for me any more than it was salvation for the disciples at Pentecost.

As we were *receivers* of His new life by faith, we now become *transmitters* of His new life by faith. Both experiences are very concrete with a distinct before and after. It is this infusion of His Spirit that abolishes the artificial sacred/secular myth. He is present in me; therefore, all of life is sacred.

This is not to say nothing is sinful. It means that sin stands out starkly and unmistakably against the pervasiveness of His presence. Godlessness is an intrusion and His presence strips and exposes it. It is naked with no camouflage. We don't force everything into an artificial sacredness. It is His sacred presence that makes me safe in the midst of a sinful world. I am "in it, but not of it." For that reason I can prophetically be His eyes, ears and voice wherever I am.

This is the Church with whom I gather. Of course we will collectively hear His voice. We hear it as we "hang out." We hear it in our worship. We hear it in the individual words of encouragement or prophecy that are given. But these don't explode in some inappropriate, emotional expostulation. There is an order for them that we understand and respect. Just as we provide for orderly fellowship, orderly worship, orderly preaching and praying, we also provide for an orderly expression of these vocal gifts of speaking in tongues and prophecy. In our congregation they are presented to and evaluated by trusted leaders among us. They judge them and decide if they are to be presented to the full congregation.

We provide orderly ways for people to be healed. It is not a special healing service, though we may have those times exclusively to pray for the sick. But every time we meet, His healing presence is with us. Healing was and is a vital part of Jesus' ministry.

All of Scripture testifies to the orderliness of God. Paul said to the Corinthian church, speaking directly about these very things, *"let everything be done decently and in order."*[56]

There are two important points to this statement: 1. "Let everything be done." Don't stop allowing the gifts to be expressed and, 2. Let them be done "decently and in order."

Weak public leadership simply decided it's too complicated to be decent and orderly. They simply refuse to allow any expression of the gifts at all in the service. Because expressions of the Holy Spirit can become embarrassing, rather than pastor them into orderliness, weak leaders relegate them to the back room or completely ignore them altogether.

The other extreme is just as bad: A weak leadership that lets *everything* be done with no decency or order. Chaos destroys the gathering. The only ones attracted are those who thrive on the

---

56 See I Corinthians 12-14 for a full discussion of this.

ensuing emotionalism. Not only do unbelievers think we are mad, most Christians do too.

The gifted, visible Jesus is the inevitable result of our ordered gathering. The power of His presence is so profound that those who have not experienced His life, love and power will find it nearly impossible to resist.

Though our gathering is primarily for the Church, often those we are touching every day will want to join us at some point. When they do, the love and acceptance they have experienced with us personally is now experienced in a collectivity of sanity and safety. One cannot experience the visible Jesus and not begin to be transformed. Of course this is a deeply emotional experience. There is joy and tears and laughter and collective expressions of praise. But it is orderly. Our leaders have explained how our emotions can be expressed in a healthy and appropriate way. There is no emotionalism. Our emotions do not rule. They do not dictate our behavior. They are an appropriate response to the fact of our love for God and for one another. They have inviolable boundaries that insure the safety and dignity of us all. Strong leadership pastors strong emotion and helps us channel it to God's glory.

If the Holy Spirit is not clearly visible when the Church gathers, He will be invisible when the Church is dispersed into the market place. As the Church experiences His intensified presence when it gathers, it will express His presence when it is apart. The two must be experienced seamlessly and never fractured or treated as independent of one another.

If you are a leader, a pastor, an influencer in the Body of Christ, then show us how this works. Incarnate what a Spirit-filled person looks and lives like. Don't hide parts of our Spirit life away in a closet. Shepherd our gifts. Don't let us be "out of order" in our lives or in our gatherings. Show us how this treasure can live in an earthen vessel. We don't need to be controlled, we need to be taught; we need an example. We have a theology of Pentecost that helps us be sane and Spirit-infused. Help us understand what this means so we can experience and express the very real presence of Christ.

To my young friend who asked, "What's the big deal?"--thank you. It was a brilliant question. I'm not sure the answer is as brilliant, but I hope it helps. What I have described is the framework of my answer. It is a point of beginning. Your generation will bring it into greater focus and effect. I have only one request as you lead His flock: Always keep these things the Big Deal they truly are.

19158470R00061

Made in the USA
Charleston, SC
09 May 2013